ALSO BY LEV TIMOFEYEV

*The Anti-Communist Manifesto:*
*Whom to Help in Russia?*

# Russia's Secret Rulers

Lev Timofeyev

# Russia's Secret Rulers

TRANSLATED BY
CATHERINE A. FITZPATRICK

WITH AN AFTERWORD BY
ANTON KOSLOV

ALFRED A. KNOPF 🐕 NEW YORK 1992

THIS IS A BORZOI BOOK
PUBLISHED BY ALFRED A. KNOPF, INC.

Library of Congress Cataloging-in-Publication Data
Timofeev, Lev.
Russia's secret rulers/by Lev Timofeyev; translated by
Catherine A. Fitzpatrick.—1st ed.
p.  cm.
ISBN 0-394-58639-5
1. Russian S.F.S.R.—Politics and government.  2. Soviet Union—
Politics and government—1985–1991.  3. Official secrets—Russian
S.F.S.R.  4. Official secrets—Soviet Union.  I. Title.
DK510.73.T56  1992
320.947—dc20  92-53188  CIP

Manufactured in the United States of America
First Edition

CONTENTS

phone would go dead as soon as we said the word "Tbilisi." We agreed to send out information about the events as if they occurred in Tambov—and then the telephone was fine; it didn't get shut off at the word "Tambov," where we said the army was killing peaceful people with sappers' shovels and poisoning them with gases. But as soon as we said "Tbilisi," the telephone would once again go dead.

Amazing technology! The professionals are now describing in the press how they installed eavesdropping equipment in apartments. They would delay the residents at work or somewhere, so that no one would suddenly return home at the wrong moment. They would open the door and enter the home wearing sneakers; strong fellows would move aside heavy furniture, cut out pieces of the wallpaper, set the microphone inside, glue it, artistically paste the wallpaper back in place, push the furniture back, and quietly disappear. Perfect!

Now they say that it's over, supposedly, that the illegal bugging has stopped. But how? How is it really done? Do they really delay us somewhere again now, enter our apartments in sneakers, and remove from the walls everything that had for years broadcast our lives "to the competent specialists"? Perhaps their property is still here, in our apartments.

But when you read in the newspapers about the training of storm troopers, of home-grown Fascists, when you read that they have special divisions prepared to seize the city waterworks or the energy system—seize them and guarantee them to work—then you begin to think that the apparatus that has burrowed into our walls will not be dormant for long, and those specialists in bugging and watching will not be idle. For example, I learned about the start of the coup of August 19, 1991, not from television news reports, but by looking out my window that morning and seeing a familiar car and KGB unit under my windows—after a two-year absence. I suppose that the bugs in the walls and ceilings of my apartment were turned on full blast that day.

It is a good thing that our children are playing today with bank notes and stocks. But what is amusement for children is alarm and tears for adults. When my wife and our two girls came to visit me in labor camp, they saw a real prison fence. They saw how soldiers brought me to the visitors' room, how the officer did not allow me even to stroke their heads or even touch them, and how the soldiers didn't let me take the piece of candy my little Katya stretched out toward me. After that, the children stopped building pretty toy prisons.

How will today's games end? Reality is such that we here in Russia, just as before, do not belong to ourselves, and know nothing about our own future.

In December 1991, on the day before his resignation, Mikhail Gorbachev had a nine-hour-long discussion with Boris Yeltsin. This was not an official rite of power transfer—there was in any case no need for such a rite, since by that time the real power was already in the hands of the President of Russia. The meeting was strictly confidential, and was called so that the head of the now-expiring USSR could pass on to his successor all the secret information he possessed: the hidden menaces, the hidden structures, the secret connections, of power. "After that meeting, I felt like going and washing myself off," Yeltsin told reporters later that same day, and his words were broadcast on all the television news programs. One would think that a person so keenly aware of the moral purity of his own political course should immediately have publicized the secrets Gorbachev had divulged that had evoked in him such evident disgust. But no, not on that day, nor after, was the content of this long conversation ever made public. Morality is one thing, but the integrity and inviolability of secret politics turned out to be stronger than the original moral impulse. And is Yeltsin so interested, after all, in having all the secret lines of power in Russia exposed to public scrutiny?

Despite the grandiose scale of aboveground political events in the former Soviet Union, their true causes, the real motivations behind them, their operative structures, and in many cases their true executors, remain in the shadows. The majority of leading Communists have rejected their old doctrine, but they appear to have done everything possible to preserve all the hidden structures of power that were created and built up during the seventy years of Communist rule.

Whether true or not, an opinion prevails widely today in Russia and the other states of the former USSR that besides the external scene of political life visible to everyone, and calculatedly presented everywhere, there is another, subterranean web of political intrigue, one inaccessible to public scrutiny and control.

Distrust of leaders, suspicion of hidden connections, corruption, and hypocrisy are so widespread that in and of themselves they exert a continual influence on the array of political forces and threaten the stability of government—whether in Moscow, Kiev, or Tbilisi. This is especially true now that people have become extremely impoverished and angered and are ready to find a scapegoat in any representative of authority.

The situation is all the more serious because the distrust and suspicion are not entirely without grounds. In each of the new states of the former USSR the power structures are genetically connected to the structures of the past, to the Communists. Everywhere in the government apparat* are people who entered politics and made their careers at a time when bureaucratic positions themselves were widely, openly bought and sold, when, in the apt expression of a former Party functionary who has since left the Party, "the very position of secretary of a district Communist Party committee presupposed the mentality of a criminal." But, without exception, all of the current government leaders were at one time or another in this or some similar post.

Can we make judgments today about the mechanism of power and the technology of the most important political decision-making without recognizing that favorable conditions for corruption not only have not vanished but have indeed increased manyfold?

---

*The apparat was the paid staff of the Party, which under the Soviet system was also the machinery of government. —TRANS.

Hundreds of billions of rubles and billions of dollars are circulating now in the criminal world in the states of the former USSR. Furthermore, it is known that *half of all profits* made in the criminal sphere are spent in bribing officials at all levels, including those of law-enforcement agencies.[1] On whom, then, do political decisions depend in the final analysis? How are they determining our future?

Many people today are completely convinced that a new hero of Russian history, as yet unknown, is changing its course in his inimitable way, and we cannot comprehend his intentions, since the protagonist himself merges with other characters. Some call him by the foreign term *mafia*. Others express themselves more plainly in Russian and label him an *ugolovnik,* a criminal, struggling for power. Still others are disposed to speak of the traits and methods of today's criminal mafia as bearing the unique stamp of yesterday's apparatchiks, KGB agents, and influential "commanders of the socialist economy," especially the chiefs of the military-industrial complex who now occupy key political and economic posts.

This undeclared "pretender to the throne" has yet to enter the political arena openly. Some believe that in the past he conducted affairs through the traditional Communist apparat—the KGB, the Ministry of Internal Affairs, the elements of the military-industrial complex. At times, he merged with them outright. Now he controls the new power structures. During all the years of President Gorbachev's tenure in office, there seemed to loom behind him a "shadow president" with unlimited power. A multilayered, well-concealed, intricately hierarchical political force developed, a force for whom, perhaps, the destruction after the failed coup of its superficial, visible, outer aspect—the structure of the Party apparat—was no great disaster.

Furthermore, serious questions arise as to whether all the crises, upheavals, and destruction of recent years might not in fact have been deliberately engineered by this political force which itself has not only escaped revolutionary disintegration but by its nature cannot even be touched by it, since that force exists on an entirely different social-political plane. Having been left intact and even strengthened, it is apparently continuing to influence government policy.

Thus, in order to find the answers to the deep conundrums that torment so many, we must recognize the reality of two levels: that of political life of recent years, and that of public opinion, which simultaneously reflects and creates it.

# CHAPTER ONE

# Making a Composite Portrait

"The role of the secret government structure is underestimated in our country now," asserts Aleksandr Kabakov, one of the most popular Russian writers of our time. "The government on the surface may surrender or not, it may fight, it is visible. . . . But there is the secret government that does not surrender, because no one can come upon it directly and call it by name—it's secret."[2]

With subtle insight into the prevailing public mood, Kabakov wrote a fantasy tale about the future, *The Defector*. In this vivid anti-utopian story, he predicts that despite the efforts of democratic politicians, the secret government (most likely the former KGB) will lead the country into a state of chaos and anarchy in order ultimately to establish a dictatorship even more brutal than Stalin's. Kabakov's tale, at first printed in a little-known journal, recently became a best-seller of its genre. Readers saw their future in the book, since, increasingly, they have grounds to suspect the presence in their country of the same kind of secret government portrayed by the writer.

Of course, it is important for us to understand the nature of any such secret government. To what extent are the official governments and well-known political figures—yesterday, Gorbachev, and today, Yeltsin, Nursultan Nazarbayev, president of Kazakhstan, and Leonid Kravchuk, the Ukrainian president, and other high-level figures—connected to it? Obviously, if they are connected, it is hardly as the planners of policy or strategy, but rather as the mere executors of strategic plans. When Western commentators speak of today's Russian politicians as people steadily perfecting the art of pulling rabbits out of hats, they miss the point that these figures themselves have likely been "pulled out of a hat," and will be stuffed back in again when the time comes, when their performance is over. There are serious grounds for such speculations.

In 1987 an acute public suspicion arose, which has not yet subsided, concerning the ban that was placed by top leaders (apparently by Gorbachev personally) on the investigation of the system of corruption in Uzbekistan. The whole country was expecting that this investigation, which began back in 1983 and was led by Special Cases Investigator Telman Gdlyan, would lead to sensational exposés implicating people in the highest circles of the governments of Uzbekistan, Russia, and other republics. But no such exposés followed. Under pressure "from above," each time that ties were discovered between Moscow and corrupt Central Asian figures, or among the highest economic and Party officials, as soon as all the pieces of the puzzle were assembled, the investigations were stopped and the criminal cases closed. The collapse of the USSR, the emergence on its territory of independent states, and the strengthening of national state structures have only increased the public's suspicion of those who have safely transferred from yesterday's structures to today's positions of power.

Gdlyan, one of the best investigators of the USSR Prosecutor's Office, was fired in 1988, as was also his close assistant Nikolai Ivanov. But their efforts to get to the bottom of things had already garnered broad public support. Both were elected to the Soviet national legislature, which gave them parliamentary immunity and saved them from arrest. Furthermore, the widespread public suspicion that the government was corrupt and tied to the underworld provided Gdlyan and Ivanov the opportunity to found their own political party.

The promise to expose the secret power structures has today become one of the most important political slogans in most, if not

all, of the states of the former USSR, especially in Russia. No
serious civic movement can get by without using this slogan.
Eduard Shevardnadze, former foreign minister and close comrade
of Gorbachev, who resigned in December 1990, has also entered
the battle against the shadow government. For that purpose
(among others) he and eight other prominent politicians have
organized the Democratic Reform Movement. "We plan measures
to eliminate the integration of the shadow structures in the new
economy, the most resolute countermeasures against attempts to
use the transition period in the interests of criminal clans," announced Shevardnadze.[3]

The intriguing thing is that no one has offered a precise description of these clans and structures. The democrats blame the corrupt
apparat, the old Party conservatives say the democrats are tied to
the mafia. Tatyana Koryagina, a prominent economist and essayist,
believes that those entangled in secret mafia ties include both Party
conservatives *and* democrats, all the way up to Gorbachev while
he was in power. Or even starting with Gorbachev, whom she was
already disposed to suspect of corruption when the future President was still secretary of the Stavropol Territory Party Committee. Whether any such old connections possibly influenced the
President's political decisions throughout his entire time in office
is a question that naturally arises when we read or hear Koryagina's fierce attacks.

As an economist, she is known for her research on the structures
of the shadow economy. She is particularly taken with the idea that
the dealers in this shadow economy, the *teneviki*,* influence political decisions in government. She is entirely certain that such
influence defined the policies of the Gorbachev regime. "The corruption of the highest levels of government first of all makes them
vulnerable to direct political blackmail and, secondly, people who
know that their hand has been in the cookie jar try to take out
insurance and try to appoint their people in all the key positions

---

*Literally, "shadow people," from the Russian word *ten*, "shadow."
—TRANS.

in government." Thus Koryagina explained her view in a conversation with the author, inevitably recalling the fact that Yeltsin in Russia, Nazarbayev in Kazakhstan, Kravchuk in Ukraine, and a number of leaders of other former Soviet republics worked at one time or another under the direct patronage of the General Secretary of the Communist Party. Despite the conflicts that have occurred, they are in a certain sense all "Gorbachev's people."[4] And if Gorbachev was tied to shadow structures, these ties necessarily extended to the present holders of power.

Koryagina has many followers and fellow believers. "Millions of people think as I do," she announces with utter assurance, and we would have to agree with her. Constantly appearing in the press, she appeals to millions with her passionate sermons on the need for moral purity in politics.

"We are not always heard," says Koryagina, "but we must shout while our strength and voices remain." Speaking at a large rally in Moscow in February 1990, she said she possessed materials showing that while President Gorbachev was secretary of the Stavropol Territory Party Committee, he had links to the North Caucasus mafia and therefore must resign, and perhaps even face trial. Soon afterward Koryagina was charged with libel and offense against the honor and dignity of the President. After six months, however, the case was closed for lack of evidence. "That means the investigation did not find any elements of slander in my words," notes Koryagina with satisfaction.

"Does that mean the court allows that such documents may exist?" I asked her. If so, perhaps they ought to be presented to the public directly?

"And how can you present them? Even today, we do not trust those power structures that should give this evidence the appropriate legal treatment. Everything all around us is rotten. All attempts to present society with the truth are immediately blocked. Papers mysteriously disappear from the offices of officials. We know that when you handle documents that are fairly innocuous in themselves but that even remotely relate to the mafia ties of the current ruling politicians, you already risk your life," claims Koryagina.

"Right now I must help a young man who at one time worked in the KGB system in one of the territories of the North Caucasus. He stumbled on some major embezzlement and bribery there, and the criminals' ties led here, to the Kremlin. . . . Then, there were 'agents' reports' which stated that the mafia had sentenced this young man to death. Now he has to be protected somehow. . . . You say that we should show documents. Well, that young man, although a former KGB worker, was still employed there as an investigator. So what can you say about the protection of witnesses? Their names cannot even be mentioned, because to do so would expose them to mortal danger."

Our generation knows only too well the danger of possessing information. In 1986, during the early days of Gorbachev's rule, at a Perm labor camp for political prisoners in the foothills of the Ural Mountains, Mikhail Furasov, a modest, very obscure engineer, died before my eyes. He was serving a twelve-year term merely because he had discovered some facts about Leonid Brezhnev that were not known to the public at large. (Brezhnev was already four years dead.) Terrorized by his arrest, investigation, and sentence, Furasov preferred to remain silent about his discoveries. But apparently they were extremely important because when he fell ill, the prison guards, hardly troubling to disguise their actions, hastened the progression of his illness and worsened his condition, finally refusing him any qualified medical aid. He was buried on the camp grounds without a marker, but with a numbered tag on his foot. And thus did Mikhail Denisovich Furasov carry with him to the grave the revelations about Brezhnev.[5]

In August 1991, under cover of the noisy street celebrations of the defeat of the neo-Communist putsch, secret Party archives were transferred from apparat files to the KGB under the control of the democratic government. Even so, there is serious doubt that we will be able to learn any details about the secret power structures. The problem is that in recent years, as if in expectation of the coming collapse, the Communists actively destroyed their files. This destruction became particularly furious in the four or five days between the Party apparat's being declared illegal and the sealing of the buildings and archives of the Central Committee and the republic and oblast Party committees. Witnesses testify that clouds of ashes from burned documents floated above the buildings housing oblast Party committees. Central television during those days repeatedly broadcast footage of garbage cans filled with shredded Party documents, fresh bonfires, and piles of still-burning embers. Even official spokesmen admit that valuable documents were destroyed.[6]

Thus it was all the more intriguing to read in a Russian newspaper the headline "Waiting in the West," with a quote from Reuters: "Western experts and political scientists are impatiently awaiting the opening of KGB files to the general public. They are particularly interested in details concerning the murder of U.S. President John F. Kennedy in 1963 and also everything connected to the [1981] attempt on the life of the Pope. They believe that KGB documents may shed light on these mysterious events." They may be waiting in the West, but in the East they are burning documents. If any people in the West expect to gain access to such secrets, I think it can only be those who lack an adequate understanding of just what has been going on in Russia during the last three-quarters of a century, and what is going on now.

Not only do documents disappear from under our very eyes but people themselves depart. On August 26, 1991, hardly had the offices and files of the Central Committee of the Communist Party on Old Square in Moscow been sealed, when N. E. Kruchina, general administrator of the Central Committee, committed suicide. Kruchina, who was in charge of all the records on the financial and economic activities of the Central Committee, jumped from the balcony of his fifth-floor apartment in a luxury Moscow building, taking with him priceless information about the secret mafia connections of the apparat. In a note he left behind, Kruchina explained that his exit was due to "fear of the future." We have to suppose that this meant fear of an impending investigation. His death, however, was so convenient for former apparatchiks that rumors about his having been murdered immediately began circulating. But the rumors were not confirmed by the investigation of the death, and some well-informed members of the former Central Committee apparat do not doubt that what took place was the fulfillment of a suicide pact—that such an exit from this life was included in advance in the list of official duties and obligations which a person accepted when he took a position involving the corporate secrets of the Party apparat. A number of other suicides of Central Committee and other officials (to be discussed later) support this speculation.

In sum, few Russians doubt that besides the visible political machinations obvious to everyone, there is another, hidden level of intrigue. The notion of the mechanism of power as a *secret* has already come into broad public awareness. Many are convinced that the details of current political intrigue will appear in newspapers and magazines only decades from now, if ever—and only to the extent that those participants in the events who remain alive will allow. Despite the policy of "glasnost," despite the liberalization of the press and the publication of memoirs by Gorbachev, Yeltsin, Yegor Ligachev, Aleksandr Yakovlev, Gavriil Popov, Anatoly Sobchak, and Raisa Gorbacheva, we still know less about contemporary Soviet politics, the mechanism of political decision-making, and the motives for the actions of contemporary politicians than we know about Brezhnev, Nikita Khrushchev, or Stalin—and even about these deceased leaders we still do not know the essential truth.

Meanwhile, few doubt that the political ties of the current rulers not only have a certain "geography" from region to region, but also their own history, from generation to generation. Today's secrets all have their roots in the past, whether recent or remote. That is precisely why attempts to gain access to the secret aspects even of past mechanisms of power have been so harshly discouraged. Secret archives have been kept tightly shut even from historians, let alone the general public. Stalin's files are housed in armored safes. No one has yet gained access to the depths of the KGB's archives. Back in the 1950s, documents casting a shadow on the political career of Nikita Khrushchev were transferred from the files of the Moscow Institute of the History of the Party to an unknown location. The archives of the Central Committee's Party Control Commission, an organ of harsh internal Party prosecutions, were removed to somewhere in the northern Ural Mountains; until quite recently they were kept closed, inaccessible even to scholars. The various purges conducted in these archives in recent decades suggest that much material which could have shed light on the secret mechanisms of political decisions has been destroyed; the reasons for this originate in the Communist regime, but continue to operate to this day.

"Don't believe anyone who brags that he knows absolutely everything about Lubyanka,"* said Vadim Bakatin, a prominent political figure, as he left his post as head of the KGB. "There is no such person. My perceptions have not changed, but have been broadened. Only now I know that I know much less about the KGB than I had previously supposed. . . . No one has ever turned the KGB upside down. At least until now." The fifty-six-year-old Bakatin had been charged with reorganizing the secret structures, but when he left his job in December 1991, he admitted he had failed: all the secret structures remained untouched.

Although there continue to be secrets, something like a criminal investigation can still be conducted. We can question witnesses, compare their testimonies with our own observations, and finally, on the basis of these possibly unrelated facts, compile at least an approximate portrait of that new protagonist in Russian political history, the "shadow president." We can assemble something akin to a police sketch, a composite portrait like those wanted posters of criminal suspects.

Can there be a police sketch that will catch Satan?

But no, we cannot know in advance which secret will be revealed, whose face will peer out at us, when we put all the available fragments of information together.

I had never looked for an entrée to such secrets until I was arrested in the spring of 1985 and accused of "anti-Soviet agitation and propaganda" for my essay "The Technology of the Black

*KGB headquarters in Moscow. —TRANS.

Market." I was jailed for two months in the same cell with Vakhab Usmanov, the Minister of the Cotton-Refining Industry in Uzbekistan, one of the leaders of the "Uzbek Party economic mafia," as he was described by the press after the trial. (Incidentally, he did not likely read very much about himself in the newspapers and magazines, since he was sentenced to death and shot by a firing squad soon afterward.) It was not that Usmanov revealed any burning secrets to me. But as I talked with him about the most ordinary matters, or reflected on his fate, I would suddenly and unexpectedly sense that leading into our cells were web-strands from warehouses, factory floors, and remote bazaars, as well as from numerous Soviet ministries, oblast Party committees, the Central Committee, the offices of Politburo members, and even Gorbachev's Kremlin office. Almost the entire country turned out to be involved.

At the time it seemed to me that these web-strands emanated merely from the economic black market, the economic mafia, and had no direct links to politics. But now that everyone else who was arrested along with Usmanov and tried for corruption has been let out of camp, I can see that this network is in fact the real mechanism of political power, a gradually developing mechanism that was formed in the course of recent decades in the bowels of the infamous Communist "administrative system." Or this system itself, based on Communist myths, was only a cover for relations and alliances that are not myths at all, but quite terrible in their real, brutal, and naked struggle for power over the country and over people. In the current era of privatization and the open market, is it not actually simpler to succeed in that struggle?

In order to try to answer these questions, we must begin far back. And now, we will let the witnesses speak.

# CHAPTER TWO

## *Witness Testimony*

# Gavriil Popov, Former Mayor of Moscow

*Gavriil Popov was elected mayor of Moscow on the same day that Boris Yeltsin became president of Russia—June 12, 1991. Only a few years earlier, Popov, then dean of the faculty of economics of Moscow State University, had been quite loyal to Communist doctrine, and supported it in his writings. Gorbachev's perestroika awakened the political animal in Popov, and he became one of the brightest democratic essayists and rally speakers, promoting political and economic liberties. He resigned from office in June 1992.*

LEV TIMOFEYEV: It is said that you became mayor because you know how to get along with the Moscow mafia.

GAVRIIL POPOV: I don't know what the Moscow mafia is. By the nature of my work, I have never encountered them. I suspect that they exist, of course, but I have had no direct contact with them. So if they are doing something and getting along somehow with the administration, then most likely this is being done behind my back. But I can state quite unequivocally that this factor is not present in my thinking and my actions.

LT: But you do suspect that the mafia exists. What kind of suspicions do you have?

GP: Well, first of all, I know the quantities of goods that come into Moscow, and at the same time I see empty stores. You know that there is a type of trade where the goods are taken to the buyers at their workplace, at the factories. We had supposed that the distributors would have enormous opportunities for theft because any factory, in order to maintain good relations with them and to get things in short supply, is inclined to make agreements and concessions.

Let's say they record that 200 pairs of shoes left for a factory, but in fact, at that factory, they sell only 150 pairs; and the rest can easily be sold by the distributors on the black market, at a higher price. This is what we thought, but when we tried to break up this system we found, to our surprise, that it was not the distributors who resisted us but the factories—the trade union leaders, those who were chiefly involved in distributing the goods within the plant. That is, the mafia lived a different kind of life than the one we thought, one that was not completely known to us.

We can only guess where the mafia operates. Let's say that in the old days, the food supply for Moscow was better even than in the nearest oblast agricultural centers like Ryazan, Tver, and others. I find it hard to believe that it was enough to publish directives about distribution—that is, merely to command the supplies. Unquestionably there was an old system of connections, and the result of their operation was that Ryazan supplied Moscow with milk, oil, cheese, and other products that are in short supply in Ryazan itself. These types of relationships can exist only on the basis of some mutual interests, agreements, deals. . . . It's even more the case today: if Moscow survives, it survives because this old system is functioning. . . . Not its old administrative, directive part, but the part that for many years has existed through some additional, shadowy agreements. Corruption was its main element. You can't suppose that people are now delivering goods to Moscow merely because they like your face. So if there isn't yet a new, normal system of open-market relations—and there isn't—that means the old, shadow, mafia system is operating.

LT: So that means that the mafia is feeding Moscow? But before, these structures were closely linked to the Party, administrative, and economic apparats. The authorities quietly supported the trade mafia and, apparently, even protected it (and themselves) with the help of the police, KGB, and army. Who is protecting it now? Or it is relying on a criminal network?

GP: I think they have two opportunities now. The first is to continue operating in the mafia mode, strengthening themselves with their own criminal associations, with racketeering. This mode is succeeding. Furthermore, apparently the criminal structures on which the trade mafia relied have in a number of cases begun functioning on their own. You have already heard about the "Chechen,"* "Solntsevo,"† and other groups.

The second opportunity is to use the new laws permitting commercial activity simply to legalize themselves—to come out of the shadows and become law-abiding participants in trade exchange. Now it is possible to open a bank, found a commodities exchange, and so on—that is, to fit within the existing legislation. So I think that the old system has been preserved, and also a new system is emerging, a system involving two approaches: one, to take advantage of the waning authority of the bureaucrats to gain greater illicit power; and the second, to enter into normal business activity. I think it's approximately like that.

LT: Do these two opportunities have some kind of political expression? Does the mafia support anyone in politics? Or perhaps they are creating their own political party? Do they have political ambitions?

GP: Among those who are legalizing themselves, political aspirations in the direction of democracy prevail. We sense this con-

*From Chechenya, an autonomous region of Russia now seeking independence. —Trans.
†Solntsevo is one of the new residential districts of Moscow. —Trans.

stantly. To the degree to which we grew stronger politically, the amount of financial aid that we received increased. During the last election, there was significant support for both me and Yeltsin. For example, leaflets and handbills that we once had to produce by hand could now be printed; many commercial printing houses were involved. In that sense there was support. According to some reports, these same forces provided help to our opponents as well. But it doesn't matter, it does no harm.

I have not noticed any significant political activity among the criminal mafia itself. I generally have the impression that these people are not very ambitious. They plan only for the short term, not the medium term. Their idea is to grab, grab, grab as much as possible. But I do wonder what prevents them from becoming normal people. What prevents them from going into regular commerce? Apparently they could not survive well in regular commerce, because they lack either the capabilities for it, or some of the necessary moral qualities. They are not involved in politics now. But under other conditions, this is the segment of the population that becomes the base for Fascist politicians—in that sense, of course, they are dangerous. Therefore everything that I am undertaking now is designed to expand the opportunities for legal business and draw as many people away from the mafia as possible—through incentives, good prospects, and opportunities for normal commerce.

LT: How real is the danger that the mafia has penetrated to the highest echelons of power?

GP: From my perspective, the penetration into the higher echelons of power is fairly great. But I don't think there's any political aspect to this. The mafia doesn't support people in the administrative structure out of adherence to some idea; it just needs a roof over its head, a fence. I can't imagine that they have their own political ambitions. Much less can I imagine that they would support some specific political ideas of a Marxist type. So if they maintain their links to an individual who swears his allegiance to Marxism, it must be for purely pragmatic reasons.

LT: Could things work the other way—that people from the old political structures might resort to the mafia's help because they wish to preserve power?

GP: Theoretically that would be possible, if in those political structures even one competent person could be found. There is complete degradation there. It's hard for me to imagine that a person could be discovered who is capable of designing a major strategic plan. If there were people like that, they would have long ago found a more effective option. One of the peculiarities of our political enemies is that they have demonstrated their utter incompetence in comprehending their own interest, at least for the near future. Before the mayoral elections in Moscow, I expected that the Communists would weigh everything and say that since they couldn't win, they would be prepared to support me under such-and-such conditions. But no, they were not capable of doing that. They could only nominate their hopeless candidate and use up their remaining strength on a lost cause. They're incapable of executing even a simple maneuver like that, and what you're talking about is a much more complicated scheme. From this point of view, the political danger of criminal structures is exaggerated. . . .

The political ambitions of businessmen are a much greater danger. But they are dangerous only in the event that they come to the conclusion that democratic forces cannot keep the country in hand. That will be a serious development. Because if the merchants, the financiers, and the businessmen believe that the democrats are not in a condition to conduct a normal life, and cannot secure a decent profit and dependably prevent strikes, then they may begin to look for a strong man. But that strong man will not be a Communist. I am certain of that.

LT: Can I draw an indirect conclusion that you trusted Gorbachev's sincerity?

GP: Gorbachev is a politician, a politician to the marrow of his bones, but not a politician of major strategic calculation. He's really a tactician, after all. It is not a question of sincerity. But Gorbachev was keenly aware of his interest and in the framework of his interest it was possible to predict his behavior and build some kind of program.

LT: Could you formulate how you see the interest that Gorbachev pursued?

GP: The same interest that pushed him toward the changes. He was too young a figure not to understand that in seven years he would have to answer for what has happened. The example of Nicolae Ceausescu in Romania was virtually enough by itself.

LT: It seems, then, that the best opportunity for him to preserve himself, his position, his life, was to support the democrats.

GP: You have to put yourself in his place. You have to understand that the democrats were alien to him. Those who surrounded him had known him for years, they were his own people. He knew what they had done for whom and when; he knew who had what ties, and so on.

LT: And all the mafia connections were known to him?

GP: Those as well. He knew how to restrain those people. But he didn't know how to restrain Popov. He had to rely on our word. From our point of view, he should have acted differently long ago. From his point of view, having the information and the archetype by which he functioned, he behaved correctly. Out of five people who came to his office, four deceived him; only the fifth would tell him a half-truth. He was getting completely one-sided, fantastically doctored information. Under those conditions, his political reactions were predetermined by his past experience and by that information. You have to give him credit: when events became critical, he found the strength within himself to go in the right direction.

His ethnic background is Cossack, a group that was relentlessly persecuted. No matter what he says about the socialist choice of his father or his grandfather, that's all nonsense, of course. He was born in a Cossack village, and from morning till night he would have heard about the executed, the murdered, the persecuted. From childhood on, he would have heard how bad things were on the collective farm and how good it was when people had their own farms. Nothing he saw from childhood on could have given him a basis for any sort of admiration or worship of this system.

Then he went to study at Moscow State University. I remember those professors, there were quite a few who were from before the revolution. We would meet and talk with them. Gorbachev's starting position in life was unquestionably such that he must have understood that the world in which he lived was unacceptable.

Then came Party work, which impelled him in the opposite direction. Aside from that work, he knew nothing. Thus a very contradictory personality was formed. His origins were on the side of complete transformation, but all his political and other habits were on the side of the existing system. That is why he had such a dichotomous model of perestroika. The combination of those two elements predetermined his actions. Even so, as a politician, he had risen in the Party under conditions of total subordination. So he thought that if he said, "You have to do it this way!" the machine would do it just that way. But he hadn't imagined that the machine would obey only within the bounds that defined its own interests. When he was forced to leave, new conditions existed, and the option of a nondemocratic development for the country no longer remained.

# CHAPTER THREE

# Who Brought Gorbachev In?

When Gorbachev retired, he not only requested that his guard be allowed to remain with him (which was done) but asked to be granted a general legal immunity. Many people saw this request as an indication that he feared the possible exposure of some criminal connections. At least, that is how it was interpreted by Boris Yeltsin, of whom the request was made. "If you are worried about something, confess now, while you are still president," he said during the nine-hour valedictory conversation.[7]

I am not pointing a finger at Gorbachev, or Yeltsin, or anyone else and claiming, "Here is the godfather of the secret political mafia." Raised in a hybrid tradition of European rationalism and Russian Tolstoyanism, I have never believed in the evil schemes of world-villains, or the intrigues of Masons, or the global network of the KGB. At the very least I have never believed in their absolute power, and have always known that in the end reason will triumph. I understand perfectly well the importance of contemporary sociological approaches to politics. But proceeding from precisely these sociological premises, we must remember that in Russia, social groups rarely influence politics in legitimate forms, accessible to the normal analysis of political scientists, in such a way that the facts of statistics and sociology can be used. Instead, the hidden, shadow, covert influence is more important; it causes more alarm and sometimes is more dangerous for the future of democracy. That is why today, when the era of Gorbachev has come to a close, it is so vital to understand who brought this great figure to power, what task he was assigned, and who supported him throughout his rule. Only then can we comprehend what legacy he has left, and to whom.

Just as it was before, Russia is currently entangled in a web of secret connections, where the interests of Party bureaucrats, the criminal world, the bigwigs of the military-industrial complex, and black marketeers are strangely interwoven. Furthermore, the borderlines of the social groups involved in this system (or who have created it, or who have been created by it) have become less and less clear; sometimes they've been completely erased. Even now, there are still reasons to wonder who is really running the country: a democratic administration; an underground network of yesterday's Party apparat; a board of directors in the military-industrial complex; the *teneviki,* the denizens of the shadow economy; or just plain criminals? Or have they all joined in one united front? No speculation here is too absurd, because the behind-the-scenes political life of Russia is so confused and unclear that anything is possible. Today's situation did not come out of nowhere. It began to take shape even before Gorbachev rose to power. In fact, Gorbachev's very political course is only a result of this process. Let us at least try to figure it out.

Many people consider it a miracle that within a few hours in August 1991, the Communist structures of power (the Party apparat, the KGB, the Union ministries) collapsed. Then, in December 1991, the whole "evil empire" came tumbling down. But no less a miracle—and a mystery at that—was the rise of Mikhail Gorbachev seven years earlier to the position of number two in the Party, and then, the following year, to the post of General Secretary.

In the official version, this miracle is almost overlooked, and the secret is barely noted. Here is the account of Raisa Maksimovna Gorbachev:

"When Chernenko died Mikhail Sergeyevich was informed immediately, and he called an urgent meeting of the Members and

Candidate Members of the Politburo and the Secretaries of the Central Committee. Decisions were taken regarding the funeral. An emergency meeting of the Central Committee was called for the next day, and at that meeting on the 11th of March Mikhail Sergeyevich was elected General Secretary of the Party Central Committee. A great deal has been written about those meetings of the Politburo and the Central Committee. All sorts of points of view, conjectures and opinions have been voiced. According to what Mikhail Sergeyevich told me, neither in the Politburo nor in the Central Committee were any other candidates put forward for the post of General Secretary. By that time the majority of the members of the Central Committee had probably arrived at a common point of view in their assessment of the situation that had arisen both in the leadership and in the country as a whole. It was a very difficult, complex situation of internal tension. Outwardly everything looked normal. Mikhail Sergeyevich's election was unanimous.

"It was late when he returned home."[8]

Everything here is deception and cover-up. In fact, nowhere has anything coherent been written about either the Politburo or the Plenum meetings. Why exactly was the internal situation in the government "tense"? Why did Gorbachev, the Politburo member in charge of agriculture, take it upon himself to convene a Politburo meeting? What is the point of speaking about common positions and unanimity when everyone remembers that no sooner did Gorbachev become General Secretary than he began a purge of the Politburo and the Central Committee? Did he really kick out his fellow believers? Nothing is comprehensible here; nothing fits together.

Let us try to understand why the situation was complicated, ambiguous, and tense.

Gorbachev was brought into the Politburo in 1979, most likely as a whipping boy. He was young and energetic. Although he had a law degree, he was considered a specialist in agriculture since he had previously held the post of secretary of the Stavropol Territory Party Committee. But being the all-powerful governor and manager of the richest grain region in the south of the country is hardly the same as having absolute power in Moscow.

Gorbachev was not yet fifty when he attained one of the highest *nomenklatura** posts, becoming a secretary of the Central Committee and a member of the Politburo. At that time, no other Party or state leader was younger than sixty; most were in fact over seventy. But despite his relative youth, the new secretary was an experienced *nomenklatura* worker. He had passed through both the posts of Komsomol† functionary and the lower ranks of the apparat. Despite his university diploma, he was familiar as well with simple peasant labor—in his student years, he had worked part-time on a combine during the harvest. Thus, objectively speaking, he was a fairly good agricultural manager.

However, the very circumstances of his career that had helped him rise to the Politburo now made it impossible for him to advance further in the Party hierarchy. The attitude toward agricultural planners was at best condescending. The Party was led either by apparat ideologues (Mikhail Suslov, Chernenko) or by protégés of the military-industrial complex (Brezhnev, Dmitry Ustinov, Yury Andropov, Andrei Gromyko). Because the perception of the USSR as a world power was connected to the military-industrial complex, it was necessary to spend more than half the gross national product on the armed forces, the munitions industry, and scientific research commissioned by the army.

Left with only pitiful remains of the government budget, agriculture has always been the most backward sector of the socialist economy; it could not bring anyone either glory or honor. All efforts to make the semiserf kolkhoz and sovkhoz‡ system of farming even partially productive were doomed. There was never enough food in the country to go around, and the per capita rate of production seemed to be forever declining. The peasants lost

---

*The *nomenklatura* is the approved list of paid Party positions, government offices, etc., and hence it is the collective term for the elite class of leaders. —TRANS.

†Young Communist League. —TRANS.

‡Collective and state farms, respectively. —TRANS.

the desire, or even forgot how, to work productively. Gorbachev's predecessor in this field was Fyodor Kulakov, who spent inglorious years in the highest Party leadership, not so much directing as pushing forward the process of complete degradation of the "socialist village." He either died of a heart attack or committed suicide after someone in the Politburo yelled at him very loudly; or perhaps, to the contrary, it was after he himself, in utter despair, screamed at one of his subordinates because of a decrease in the number of cattle or an insufficient production of buckwheat. He was forgotten the day after his funeral.

No doubt a similar fate awaited Gorbachev as well. Subsequently, he himself acknowledged his subordinate position in the Politburo in coarse but candid language: "You don't pity [Viktor] Chebrikov. You don't love Ligachev," he told Vitaly Korotich, editor-in-chief of the democratic journal *Ogonyok*. "But all of us licked Brezhnev's ass together. All of us!"[9]

Gorbachev's position was all the shakier given that he was automatically assigned responsibility for fulfilling a totally unrealistic and purely propagandistic Food Program, in which the Party leaders incessantly repeated the customary imperative forms of the verbs "oblige," "raise," and "strengthen," avowing in triumphal tones that, at long last, the kolkhozes and sovkhozes would produce enough grain, milk, meat, and vegetables to feed everyone.

The Food Program was proclaimed by Brezhnev when he was already senile and near the end. Yet no one had any notion that the aged leader's death was imminent; he seemed at the time to be eternal. It was far more logical to suppose that the young Gorbachev had been brought in so that when, in time, the Food Program failed—and fail it would, inevitably, since it did not include any reforms of the kolkhoz-sovkhoz system—he, Gorbachev, could be ostentatiously removed as the culprit in the failure. But it would appear that someone in the Brezhnev entourage who knew that little time remained for the aged General Secretary must have had other ideas for this youngest member of the Politburo.

. . .

I fear we will never learn the whole truth about the motives for decisions concerning personnel and leadership succession in the Brezhnev-Chernenko era. There has never been anything of this sort in the official documents of the Central Committee and the Politburo. No reasons were recorded when someone was removed from his post. Even if one of the leaders of that time had dared to keep an intimate diary (which is hard to imagine), most likely such a document would have long since disappeared into the bowels of the KGB.

No doubt the scandal that broke out over Khrushchev's memoirs, which had slipped through the fingers of the KGB and were published in the West, forced the Chekists* to be even more vigilant. The members of the Politburo would never have risked entrusting their intimate thoughts to paper. Knowing the morals of their colleagues, none of them could feel safe.

The relations among those in the Politburo were always an enormous secret—especially where the process of inheriting power was concerned. The intrigues that were woven there never surfaced until one of the former leaders was declared an "enemy of the people" or some other type of criminal and sent into ignominious obscurity—or, under Stalin (and for a time after him), executed by firing squad. It was by intrigue that in 1964 Nikita Khrushchev was removed. In the same way, he had in his day removed from the political scene Stalin's famous comrades-in-arms—Vyacheslav Molotov, Lazar Kaganovich, Georgy Malenkov, and the great military commander Georgy Zhukov. Earlier, Khrushchev had staged the arrest and execution of the omniscient Lavrenty Beria, the chief of Stalin's secret police. The public learned about the changes in the corridors of power only after they had all been made. Even today, we have only indirect sources of

*A nickname, still used today, derived from *ChK,* the Russian acronym for the Extraordinary Commission for Fighting Counterrevolution and Sabotage, the Bolshevik precursor of the KGB. —TRANS.

information to guide us in reconstructing the hows and whys of the most important political decisions of that era.

An old Party figure joked gloomily back in the 1920s that even after the Bolsheviks became the ruling party, they simply could not leave the underground. The truth of these words has become increasingly obvious in our own time, as the deeply hidden mechanisms of the Communist Party's activities have been gradually revealed. And the more that has been revealed, the more speculation there has been about what is still locked up and concealed and even about what will never be unearthed completely. Many people are convinced that, in the final analysis, we shall never learn more about the Communist ruling structures than what they let us learn.

We return to our examination into the secrets surrounding the transfer of power in the Politburo near the end of the Brezhnev era. We may never learn what thoughts were in the minds of the patriarchs of that era, what discussions were held by what people in dachas outside Moscow preceding the appointment of Gorbachev, and the very ritual itself of secret meetings by which important decisions were made. But we can, at least in part, imagine these rituals.

In his essay "Metacorruption,"* the young scholar Anton Koslov quite properly notes the genetic similarities between the ruling structures of the Communist Party and the mafia structures of the recent and even distant past. In fact, we cannot understand who Gorbachev was unless at least to some extent we come to know, if not the content, then the atmosphere, of the highest structures of government at that time.

The apparat's style of work depended on the General Secretary, who was so incapacitated that many observers felt he could hardly act as a leader. In reality, the country was being run by other people. "Most likely, behind Brezhnev there was some kind of informal group drawn from the Politburo, but not only from there, and it was this group that directed Soviet policy in his name,"

---

*See Afterword. —TRANS.

believes Eduard Gierek, who was leader of Poland at the time and frequently met with Soviet higher-ups. "No one paid attention to Brezhnev; no one heeded his opinion. The people running the country in Brezhnev's name did not want to permit the exposure of the leader himself, nor their role in all this."[10] While Western political scientists often called the Soviet government gerontocracy, Soviet dissidents coined a harsher, more precise term: necrocracy, rule by the dead.

The three men who had particularly strong influence on the half-dead Brezhnev were Mikhail Suslov, chief ideologue of the Party and its "gray cardinal," who had been close to the summit of power even under Stalin; Yury Andropov, chairman and later chief overseer of the KGB, who many believe possessed secret dossiers on all his colleagues in the leadership of the country and Party; and Konstantin Chernenko, who controlled the selection and placement of the highest Party cadres.

Chernenko was particularly influential in the Party's apparat. He was a longtime comrade of Brezhnev's who had climbed the rungs of the Party career ladder from modest functionary of the Moldavian Central Committee to powerful secretary of the Party in Moscow. He never tried to thrust himself into leadership, but was promoted on account of various personal services provided to Brezhnev. Even then, near the apex of the Party pyramid, he preferred to remain in the shadows and operate quietly. Chernenko was able to do so because subordinate to him was the Special Department of the Central Committee, which possessed all Party secrets; the most important Party documents, including compromising material on Politburo members, flowed through this department.

Two other men were part of Brezhnev's immediate circle: Dmitry Ustinov, the defense minister, and Andrei Gromyko, the foreign minister. Both had been in Stalin's cabinet, and were very closely connected to the influential elite of the military-industrial complex. It is believed that these five constituted, with Brezhnev, the political power of the country; only one of them, of course, could be General Secretary.

"The members of the Politburo gathered for meetings in the Kremlin on the third floor of an old building with high ceilings and high windows, overlooking the Kremlin wall," wrote one of the "young" members of the highest body of Communist power, the sixty-five-year-old Yegor Ligachev, in 1991. "Red Square and the Lenin Mausoleum were nearby. . . . all types of communication lines have been installed. This building contained the Politburo conference hall, the Kremlin office of the General Secretary and his waiting room, as well as the so-called Walnut Room, which had a large, round table at which members of the top political leadership exchanged opinions before the sessions. Here preliminary discussions, unofficially, without minutes or a transcript, would go on about the most important and most complicated issues on the agenda. At times the actual session would not begin at 11:00 on the dot, but fifteen or twenty minutes later. Candidate members of the Politburo and the Central Committee secretaries also took part in the meetings, but they would go directly to an oblong hall and take their regular (unofficial) places at a long table. Guests were seated at small tables along the wall.

"In the last years of the Brezhnev era, Politburo meetings were short and rapid-moving—within an hour, sometimes forty minutes, prepared decisions were passed, and everyone would go home."[11]

The General Secretary would preside at Politburo sessions. To his right was the place of the number-two man in the Party, who chaired the sessions in the absence of the General Secretary. He would inherit power if the General Secretary were to die.

Actually, the number two in the Party did not assume power immediately—even he needed a few hours or days in order to gain his right. That is why reports of the death of a General Secretary were never made right away; the official announcement of the death of Brezhnev, for example, was made more than twenty-four hours after the fact. When Andropov, the General Secretary after Brezhnev, died on February 9, 1984, the secretaries of oblast Party committees didn't learn the news until coded cables arrived twelve hours later. But among those who really claimed power, maneuvers concerning its transfer began as soon as the eyes of the current leader were closed. Within a few minutes of the death of Andropov, Gorbachev, then a Politburo member, called his colleague Ligachev in Tomsk:

" 'Yegor, there's been a misfortune. Andropov has died. Fly back here. Be in Moscow by tomorrow morning, you're needed here. . . .'

"The official coded message about Andropov's death didn't reach the Tomsk Province Party Committee until the next morning."[12]

From January 1982 until March 1985, the funerals of Politburo members came in rapid succession: Suslov, Brezhnev, Andropov, Ustinov, and finally Chernenko. It was as if from time to time some invisible hand would make the sign of the cross over this pack of specters, and the next phantom would crumble into ashes. The deceased leaders were buried behind Lenin's Mausoleum on Red Square at the Kremlin Wall. Each time, there was great pomp and circumstance, with farewell speeches, a gun carriage carrying the coffin or the urn, and a military salute. Only a few select individuals would be allowed at the ceremony. Ordinary people, who had not the slightest respect for this decrepit lot, joked morosely that it would make sense to issue a permanent pass for funerals.

But despite the showy nature of the ceremony, people understood that this was not a frivolous affair and, peering at the television screen, noted to themselves in which order the Politburo members followed behind the coffin, and in which order they stood at the honor guard. The unchanging ritual of the funerals bore witness to the existence of a secret but invincible ritual of the inheritance of power: the first person to walk behind the coffin was invariably the one who would be declared General Secretary a few hours later.

In fact, the number-two man inevitably inherited power—even if this contradicted common sense. When Andropov died in February 1984, Chernenko became General Secretary, despite the fact that he was already mortally ill with emphysema. Some commentators who were close to the Politburo have dismissed rumors to the effect that Andropov wanted Gorbachev as his successor. In their view, any attempt to change the *ritual* of the inheritance of power would have been perceived by the ancient inhabitants of the Politburo as an attack on the very *system* of power. Understandably, Defense Minister Ustinov and his loyal troops would have immediately had a decisive say in the matter.

Gorbachev's path to the highest post in Party and state could start only from the number-two slot. But what is most inexplicable, even mysterious, is that after becoming General Secretary, Konstantin Chernenko was able to insist successfully that Gorbachev become the Central Committee secretary who would be granted the honor and power to chair the Central Committee Secretariat meetings, and in Chernenko's absence, sessions of the Politburo itself. At the very beginning, then, of the rule of the fatally ill, all-but-doomed Chernenko, our hero becomes his official successor. This is how Ligachev, who was present at the Politburo meeting, describes it:

". . . at an organizational meeting of the Politburo, Chernenko proposed assigning Gorbachev to chair the meetings of the Central Committee Secretariat. Chernenko apparently understood that an energetic, youthful, and physically strong person was needed for this.

"However, not all the members of the Politburo held such a sane point of view. [Vladimir] Tikhonov immediately reacted to the General Secretary's proposal:

" 'Well, Gorbachev will turn the Secretariat meetings into a collegium of the Ministry of Agriculture, and will push only agricultural issues there.'

"Clearly, this was only a formal pretext to dismiss Gorbachev's candidacy, but someone else immediately took it up and there were several other remarks expressing doubt. But Marshal Ustinov spoke up in favor of the General Secretary's proposal.

"And then, Gromyko, making use of his diplomatic experience to dissipate the tension that had arisen, took the floor. He proposed a Solomonic solution: 'Let's give this some thought, let's not be hasty. We'll come back to this question later.'

"But, the rather phlegmatic Chernenko, with his weak health, suddenly displayed some character, and said firmly:

" 'Nevertheless, I am going to insist that you support my proposal to entrust the chairing of the Secretariat to Comrade Gorbachev.' "[13]

Why Gorbachev? It would seem that there were far more influential people in the Politburo at that time, people who had held both the visible and the secret reins of power: for instance, Viktor Grishin, secretary of the Moscow City Party Committee, a figure who by general admission was close to the mafia; or Grigory Romanov, formerly the powerful secretary of the Leningrad Oblast Committee, a man who was not yet old, no less energetic than Gorbachev, and quite strong physically. Thus, in Ligachev's memoirs there is a plain hint at some secret intrigue which brought Gorbachev to power. By 1992, having gotten to know Gorbachev as a genius at big-time political games and intrigue, we are inclined to accept as the truth Ligachev's scenario for Gorbachev's path to power. Although we must suppose that the battle was waged not only at the level of verbal skirmishes at the meeting table.

The real, secret war behind the scene was waged not for life, but to the death. Eduard Shevardnadze has reported that in 1984 officials of the Ministry of Internal Affairs were ordered at any cost to dig up compromising material on Gorbachev from the Stavropol period of his career. (Are these the same people about whom Tatyana Koryagina is so concerned?) The rivals understood that defeat meant, if not physical death, then rapid political death.

Gorbachev, perfectly familiar with the rules of the game and the size of the stakes, turned out to be more adroit than his rivals in respect to, among other things, the ability to find compromising material. No sooner did he become General Secretary than he headed off to Leningrad, where he publicly accused his more energetic rival, Romanov, of corruption and abuse of his official position. (Rumors spread that one of the accusations was that when Romanov was secretary of the Leningrad Oblast Party Committee, he borrowed from a museum a set of china that had belonged to the tsars to serve guests at the wedding of his daughter to Anatoly Karpov, the world chess champion. This is one of the folkloric versions of the story of the battle for power, but folklore always romanticizes events and weaves them into the fabric of everyday life. We do not know if the museum service was used or even if there actually was a marriage between the secretary's daughter and the chess champion, but what is known is that after taking the job of chairing the Politburo sessions under Chernenko, Gorbachev, whether deliberately or by happenstance, forced Romanov out of that role, eliminating his most dangerous political enemy.) Grishin soon followed Romanov into political oblivion.

But in a conversation with the author, Shevardnadze presented his own version of the mechanics of Gorbachev's nomination. It was not sudden—and therefore inexplicable and mysterious—but gradual, logical, and even necessary that Gorbachev be nominated. And he had already virtually become number two in the Party under Andropov. "Actually, there was no such overt ranking—number two, number three," recalls Shevardnadze, who was a candidate member of the Politburo at the time. "Gorbachev was already being given many assignments. Andropov himself gave him many assignments, including some that went beyond the bounds of the agricultural-industrial complex. We essentially considered him then the number two under Andropov. . . . When Andropov died, Chernenko was faced with a fait accompli. He was forced either to seek to change this existing array of forces—and thus enter into conflict with Gorbachev, who had already been recognized as the number two—or to reconcile himself to the state of affairs and support it. . . . Therefore, I'm not sure that Chernenko really treated Romanov or someone else with much respect."

The picture painted by Shevardnadze directly contradicts the testimony of Ligachev and several other memoirists. If, as they claim, Chernenko had to push for Gorbachev's nomination, it hardly follows that under Andropov Gorbachev was granted broad authority and even then was recognized as number two. Here it would be especially important to know not only *how* Gorbachev came to power but what he brought with him. Could anyone have known what policy the new leader would offer the country?

"Some people already knew then," says Eduard Shevardnadze, "and some were just plain afraid. They know that Gorbachev— even under Brezhnev, especially under Andropov, and then under Chernenko as well—had developed as a reformer. A reformer and a man who was capable of getting his own way, capable of stubbornly pushing the line in keeping with his own beliefs. The relatively young generation in the Politburo—to which [Nikolai] Ryzhkov and I belonged—knew this."

Who feared Gorbachev, and why? Actually, were they not right to be afraid? But did Gorbachev himself subsequently understand well what he was doing, and do it deliberately? Did he realize the consequences of even a partial liberalization of the press and television, and proceed anyway? Did he really understand what he was doing when in 1988 he proposed a new electoral law permitting several candidates to be nominated for a given post? Did he understand as he embarked on that course that even the slightest form of competition, in either politics or the economy, would inevitably lead to a complete collapse of Communist doctrine? Any freshman political scientist could have told him it was inevitable. But did the very experienced Andropov, Chernenko, Ustinov, and others who had blessed him want this from him? It is hard to believe that these people, so exquisitely skilled in banning and bloodily suppressing any degree of freedom, could have desired the liberation of the country by him.

The very list of leaders supporting Gorbachev provides evidence that the KGB and the Soviet military-industrial complex were the chief forces behind him. Today we know that, at the beginning of the 1980s, even many within the military-industrial complex were coming to share the conviction, already widespread in the country at large, that the economy, including the defense sector, was heading for a profound crisis—and in that conviction were willing to consider reforms that might avert the crisis. But if we suppose that Gorbachev started his rise to power as a man of the military-industrial complex, then we must admit that by the beginning of the next decade this same complex had become Gorbachev's chief enemy. It was these forces, including some of the President's closest aides, who staged against him the abortive coup of August 1991.

Despite having been a protégé of Andropov's, Gorbachev rejected in toto his patron's harsh style of administrative rule. He supported the idea of free enterprise and consistently created favorable conditions for the free flow of capital in the USSR (including capital that had been hoarded by the dealers on the black market and in the shadow economy).

No matter how we approach the fact of the last General Secretary's rise to power, everything is filled with contradictions that clearly do not fit. So who is Gorbachev, after all? A subtle tactician, carrying out profoundly secret programs, or a clever opportunist and brilliant political intriguer, propelling the country toward change while seeking to maintain power under any change of course, even the most drastic?

We do not know the precise motives for Mikhail Gorbachev's actions. What we do know is that he is someone who emerged from the depths of the Party *nomenklatura* and Party apparat. Then we can raise a more general question: What is the moral and professional character of a bureaucrat who not only spent decades in the Party apparat, but made a dizzying career?

One of the most widespread arguments of Gorbachev's political enemies is that there could be no honest people at all in the Party structures. All of them were involved in corruption; otherwise, this argument goes, it would be impossible for them to have careers. This line of thinking deserves serious examination. But more important than how Gorbachev behaved in the 1970s is what exactly influenced his political behavior and his decisions of recent years.

CHAPTER FOUR

*Witness Testimony*

# Eduard Shevardnadze, Former Foreign Minister and Politburo Member

*Eduard Shevardnadze climbed all the rungs of the Communist apparat ladder: First Secretary of the Georgian Komsomol Central Committee; Minister of Internal Affairs; First Secretary of the Georgian Communist Party Central Committee; candidate member of the Politburo; Politburo member; Foreign Minister. He was one of Gorbachev's closest fellow believers in the early period of perestroika. After the overthrow of the authoritarian Georgian president Zviad Gamsakhurdia in January 1992, Shevardnadze was called back to his homeland to head the interim government.*

LEV TIMOFEYEV: In the present political lineup of opposing forces, whose team are you on?

EDUARD SHEVARDNADZE: I believed in Stalin, believed in Khrushchev, then was disenchanted, then believed in Brezhnev. Parallel to this, serious doubts appeared. The higher I rose in my own republic, the more these doubts intensified. By the beginning of the 1980s, I had come to the conclusion that everything was rotten in this system. I even spoke of this with Gorbachev; he later publicly recalled this conversation. "Everything is rotten; everything has to be changed."

LT: What exactly was rotten? Do you mean corruption in the Party apparat?

ES: No. The system. The system was rotten. At that time—ten years ago—I was not yet saying that the system was built on fallacious principles from the very beginning, but I saw that we had come to a dead end and had lost our bearings. . . .

LT: What were your conversations with Gorbachev about at the beginning of the 1980s? What was their tone? Were they just friendly chats between two high-ranking politicians, or did you already have some aim for the future?

ES: No, we didn't draft any political programs. We didn't plan that we would come and take power tomorrow and would rule in accordance with our program—Gorbachev had no such ambitions, and I even less. These were the talks of two comrades. We had known each other a long time, ever since our days in the Komsomol. Gorbachev usually took his vacations in Georgia. We rode around the republic and talked a lot. . . .

Once I introduced him to a remarkable peasant family. The father was an injured war veteran, probably in his sixties. The grandchildren lived with him and his wife. And this family kept fifteen cows. I brought Gorbachev there so that he could take a look at a Soviet *kulak*.* Fifteen cows! The kolkhoz had set aside a field for him, and he scythed the grass where they pastured. The family sold the milk to the kolkhoz. Then we wondered what we should do. It would not take much brains to *dekulakize*† him. All we had to do was call in the police inspector and that would be that. But then there'd be no milk, either. All right, you allowed this pasture in one district and even started to help them; but the other districts, and the rest of the country? The existing system would not allow you to turn over every kolkhoz this way. (Later, in the course of perestroika, conditions for this type of work began to be created.) But in those days, every time we allowed such an experi-

---

*Literally "fist," *kulak* is the Soviet term for wealthy peasants who were massacred during collectivization in the 1920s and 1930s. —TRANS.
†A euphemistic term for the persecution of *kulaks*. —TRANS.

ment, we were dragged before the Central Committee: "Explain what this is all about: capitalism or socialism?" One kind Central Committee worker once said to a colleague of mine: "My dear fellow, we need meat, we need milk, but we can't depart from Marx." The totalitarian system restricted a person, put him within strict bounds.

LT: But was it really a totalitarian system? There was no open market in the country, but there was always the black market, where you could get anything that was in short supply. . . . Corruption of the apparat, the black market, the shadow economy. All of that, thank God, destroyed the system from inside. . . . It seems that the Soviet experience proves that no totalitarian system can survive for long. You cannot stifle a person with prohibitions—he will always find a loophole in order to survive. . . . Was corruption widespread in Georgia?

ES: You know, I have a fair amount of experience fighting corruption. I devoted fifteen years of my life, if not more, to this problem. I was forced to work, against my will, in the appropriate agencies.

LT: Were you the chairman of the KGB?

ES: No, Minister of Internal Affairs. I categorically refused, but it was customary to submit to Party discipline. And then, when I headed the Party organization of the [Georgian] republic, I sincerely believed that I could eradicate corruption; I thought that justice would triumph if someone honest and unafraid to wage this battle was the head of the republic or an institution. There were some results: corruption decreased. But I finally became convinced that this struggle did not attract the effort it should because corruption, bribe-taking, and abuse of office were all interrelated. As long as there was a shortage of goods, food, and services, no matter how harsh the laws and how brutal the law-enforcement officers, evil would not be eradicated. I sought the sources for these ills and found them in the system itself. It was the conservatism in the economy, the centralized system, the monopoly on property. It was the monopoly of one party on power—and that influences the economy, of course. The individual, the chief subject of economic life, is pushed into the background.

LT: For fifteen years, you fought corruption and the mafia. Have these lessened at all?

ES: No, probably not. We are now in a transitional phase, one that's dragged on a lot. It is natural that new forces are coming on to the scene now. Among them are people who have a vested interest in progress, both personally and in terms of the interests of society. But mafiosi are also appearing on the scene, as you have said. And we are once again betting on the administrative approach, once again passing new laws—limiting the cooperatives, restricting entrepreneurs and property owners. You will never get far with that. We need economic incentives and economic legislation. In the process of creating economic incentives a new sort of person will be formed, a producer, entrepreneur, or executive who is vitally interested in the success of the cause and in the final results.

LT: During the period of your battle with the mafia, how high up did the mafiosi penetrate the agencies of power?

ES: Even now they are sitting in all the structures.

LT: To what extent can they influence politics?

ES: In those days, they were in all the Party bodies. Some of them were exposed and punished, and some were fired or relocated. You would know that someone was a bribe-taker, but you couldn't prove it. But people knew everything. Some halfhearted measures were taken. It would happen that you would say to such a person: "We know what you are up to. Resign before it's too late!" I once collected about 100 or 150 people and I knew that they had embezzled millions. And I threatened that we would catch them. "You have children, families, and friends, comrades; finally, you have the Motherland," I told them. "That's enough now. You've been accumulating all these years. Stop it!" They understood that there was a kind of humanism in this approach, and they did leave—they resigned and left their "fields," so to say.

LT: Are people saying that the influence of mafia structures on political life has now increased?

ES: Well, the more restrictions on the economy, the more opportunities for the mafia. We need more freedom. I believe that any harsh restrictions or any limitation on profits will not lead to good practices.

LT: You are a diplomat and therefore you have diplomatically not answered my question. But here I'm a reporter. Here are the lines of corruption that lead from the shadow economy and, to a lesser extent, from the downright criminal world—to what level of political power do they lead? How much do they influence political decisions? How high does it go, and are they at every level? To what extent do these connections entangle the current system of government?

ES: I will not answer directly, because I see the reasons behind the question. While there are these reasons—while the right conditions exist—it is impossible to stop corruption. Corrupt elements can be found in the Supreme Soviet, among deputies, and at the level of ministers, not to mention the municipal authorities. You have to create the conditions so that a person has a vested interest in the final outcome of his labor. This interest is the best check on morality.

# CHAPTER FIVE

*Witness Testimony*

# Zviad Gamsakhurdia,
# Former President of Georgia

*Zviad Gamsakhurdia, son of the prominent Georgian writer Konstantin Gamsakhurdia, was formerly a dissident and political prisoner. After rising to power in 1991 in a democratic election, he displayed a brutal intolerance toward both the national opposition and national minorities; this led to armed conflicts throughout the Georgian republic. The President's followers emphasize his uncompromising position in the battle for the complete independence of Georgia. His opponents point instead to an act of betrayal in the early 1980s: after being arrested for anti-Communist activity, Gamsakhurdia appeared on television to recant and confess; this helped him to avoid the usual harsh punishment meted out to dissidents.*

*In January 1992, a prolonged siege by armed insurrectionists forced Gamsakhurdia to go into hiding. He continues to direct loyal troops against the government, but the republic's provisional military rulers have prevented him from reassuming power. Today, Georgia remains the scene of unceasing political battle that repeatedly spills over into armed conflict.*

LEV TIMOFEYEV: The government has changed in Georgia. The Communists are gone. But did they turn over everything that they had run? Did they give back everything that they had owned until now?

ZVIAD GAMSAKHURDIA: I will describe everything to you in detail. Back in 1990, the Communists saw that they were facing defeat. A popular nationalist movement arose, everyone united against them, and elections were prepared. We began to fight for a democratic electoral law and resorted to strikes. And we won! As soon as they saw that the law was passed, they began to mobilize the mafia. The mafia are the directors of large factories, the heads of the agricultural-industrial complex. These people are really the mafia. They extract all the money and resources out of the peasants and deal with millions. They extract it in the form of bribes and by inflating production figures. The flow of these millions or billions of rubles was managed by the Party boss, the deputy chairman of the Soviet of Ministers, whose name is Mgeladze. He purchased his position. He was Shevardnadze's man—you can say that Shevardnadze legalized this mafia. He has a reputation for fighting the mafia, but in reality, he's in with them.

LT: But finally, you beat them and became president. So was the battle with the mafia over?

ZG: No, I couldn't beat them. We beat the Communist Party. But the Communist Party is only the outer screen, they were behind it in the shadows. Even now, every day we fire them from their positions. We expose someone and fire him. But there are so many of them, we can't keep up.

LT: How do you expose them?

ZG: I see that a person who is engaged in sabotage continues to rob the state, and a dossier comes in on him. . . .

LT: In what form does this dossier come?

ZG: In different ways. I mean a dossier from the KGB—the KGB is now ours. It does not exist as a political police; I have it as a regular police. You understand? I kicked everyone out of there who was a collaborator with Moscow. I cleaned things out a bit. A dossier comes in through the finance ministry, from the financial inspector. But it is impossible to control everything, because the mafia is everywhere. You can practically say that we're stuck in this swamp. It's a hydra with many heads.

LT: It looks as if the mafia virtually runs everything. What next? How can you take this power away from them?

ZG: I don't know. I'm very pessimistic. They try to buy my parliament and my ministries. They're buying them right out from under me. Rumors reach me that even among my closest aides there is bribe-taking. They have penetrated this far. And their bosses are in Moscow. Mgeladze, this man who has now fled Tbilisi, is a criminal before the people (his name means "wolf"). Guram Mgeladze. He is in Moscow now; he was given a place in the local agricultural-industrial complex, because *Batyushka** is defending him. Mgeladze was his main agent in Georgia.

LT: *Batyushka* is Gorbachev?

ZG: Of course, he is number one. . . . There is a campaign against me in Moscow—they call me a Fascist, a Khomeini. In the newspapers—here, you can see—I am supposed to be like Hitler. This is the mafia at work. And Mgeladze provides the money. He accumulated several millions and nominated his own candidate to the post of president. He's a man of the Kremlin. He himself is an economist, a professor. They wanted to promote him, but the people have seen through him. The people know—they know everything. But I am still powerless before him.

LT: In three years or so, in whose hands will all the property of Georgia be?

*Literally "little father," a term of respect used in the sense of "the Godfather," which Gamsakhurdia is employing here ironically. —TRANS.

ZG: Well, that's just what I'm afraid of, that once again it will be in their hands. Now, like jackals, they have opened their jaws and are waiting for the law on privatization to be passed. As soon as there is a law on privatization, they will jump on everything. Try to figure out now who is who. I do not know all their names, there are tens of thousands of them. Therefore, I want the law on enterprises and privatization to be very strict—not the way it is in the West. What do they care over there? They don't have this problem. They have an honest entrepreneurial class; entrepreneurs are neither enemies of their people nor agents of a foreign power.

In their hands, enterprise serves good, serves the people. But these people, how do I know where a person has come from? They will take an enterprise, a factory, and gradually buy all the property. And once again they will strangle us.

LT: But each entrepreneur will obey the laws of the market—if, of course, he's acting on his own behalf and isn't a figurehead serving some structure. Isn't that so?

ZG: But the structure could be invisible.

There is a certain underground clan. Wolves sense one another, and this is a wolf's clan, where everyone understands each other, where they all support one another. They have their officials in the government—despite my principled nature and unprecedented purge, for which they hate me. This mafia will once again surface if privatization is uncontrolled. That is why I want to establish strict government control—a committee for state control to put everything in its place, and to look at the character of each person who claims property.

LT: What do you mean—"put everything in its place"?

ZG: There will be practical control, inspection. We have invited very few people—only honest people, especially among women. There are those who are not susceptible to that damned money—people for whom Georgia is dear, for whom our freedom is dear.

These kinds of people must be gathered and government control must be established.

LT: Government control over the process of privatization?

ZG: Absolutely. Without that, we will perish.

LT: And how will it be done?

ZG: It will be done. It was done in Lithuania, after all. Despite the fact that Lithuania was the most anti-socialist country, it was done. Control is needed (without it I cannot carry out privatization); it is the only salvation from the mafia. The only salvation. Now they no longer have any political force, but they have enormous economic power. And economic force is the basis for politics. Therefore, they aren't losing hope. But they have no authority. They don't have the personality to oppose me. . . . They have tried, and five candidates were brought out [during the elections]. One received 1 percent, another received 2 percent, and another—the most popular among them—received 7 percent.

LT: What kind of structure does the mafia that opposes you have?

ZG: The elite that runs things, the managers, is pure Party. The middle level is commercial. These are directors, distributors, and technicians. These are millionaires. Fruits, wine—all of this means enormous amounts of money. Their wealth is the result of deception, inflating production figures, giving incorrect change, putting fingers on the scale, and falsifying the numbers.

LT: Many suspect that the KGB and the mafia are connected. It is known that the KGB has many informers. But now the Georgian KGB, it appears, is subordinate to you.

ZG: Not completely. A part of it is subordinate, a small part. And the rest still serves Moscow. Besides, now they are like a revolving door in a department store—when I want to, I open it; when Moscow wants to, they open it. I squeeze my information out of them, Moscow squeezes its information. In fact, I know that the majority of them are traitors.

LT: Have they given you lists of informers?

ZG: No, they haven't, although I've demanded it. I said that if you don't reveal that list for me, then I will declare war. They are afraid of Moscow. They are servants of two masters, and servants of two masters are always afraid. But I'm gradually putting them under my control.

LT: What will you do when they reveal the list of informers?

ZG: I think I won't publicize it. I want to bring the Church into it, so that the informers could go to confession, and then I will forgive them their past. But if they continue in the future, no, I won't forgive them. There is no other option—there are 40,000 informers.

LT: And you call the people that they serve a mafia? I don't envy you.

ZG: Even now it is very dangerous. I don't know what they will do tomorrow. I myself don't know. It's as if I'm sitting on a volcano. It's a very bad position.

LT: But you have 90 percent of the voters with you. And if privatization goes successfully in Russia, then will it be easier for you?

ZG: Of course. We will then breathe a sigh of relief. Our mafia are Moscow's people.

# CHAPTER SIX

# The Mafia: Uzbek Evidence

As I have said, I don't know exactly when Vakhab Usmanov was executed by firing squad. Usmanov, the Minister of the Cotton-Refining Industry in Uzbekistan, was tried in August 1986, almost a year after we'd shared a cell in Lefortovo Prison. I had served the first months of my six-year term of strict-regimen labor camp for "anti-Soviet agitation and propaganda" when I read in the newspaper that the former minister had been sentenced to death. I clearly imagined and even partly sensed the hysteria and cold horror that very likely seized Vakhab at the moment sentence was pronounced.

Back in Lefortovo, he had anticipated death, and spoke of the future with grief and fear. We, his cellmates, had to calm him every day, sometimes several times a day, assuring him that they would let him off, or, if not, that the most he would get would be nine or ten years of labor camp, but probably even less. Sometimes he would ask us to play guessing games and we would play a game of throwing our fingers and guess five or six. We pitied him and tried in many ways to keep him from getting depressed.

Later, reading the newspaper announcement, I was able to think of only one explanation for the harsh sentence: a genuine campaign against corruption had been launched. Following on this Uzbek Cotton Affair, after the execution of the minister, we would hear about other cases and other executions of high republic officials. But no campaign followed.

Why did they execute Usmanov? After all, he was no deliberate and hardened evildoer, no murderer or rapist. Even given the type of crimes of which he was accused (bribe-taking and inflating production figures), it was clear upon careful scrutiny that he could not have been the leader of a criminal gang. Surely the investigators analyzing the economic and political mechanisms of the crimes could realize that it was a question of a republicwide (at the very least) *system* of corruption. And by Usmanov's position in the power structure, there had to be at least ten other republic leaders who were more influential, and much more responsible than he would be as an industrial minister.

No matter how much I thought about the case, reading and rereading the brief announcement, I could not discern any reasonable explanation for the execution of Vakhab Usmanov. It seemed as if this unfortunate minister had been deliberately singled out, marked with a fateful circle, and so this death by firing squad acquired the nature of some especially significant yet mysterious act.

We have lived our lives in the mysterious world of socialism. We never knew who was really running the country, who was making the political decisions, who was determining our fates, and to whom our lives belonged. What is mysterious in this world is not only what is secret, but also what everyone can see which isn't comprehensible and isn't studied. Not only is it not studied, but it is everywhere deliberately and falsely portrayed; the farther the lie spreads, the more mysterious is that which we take for granted.

Everyone is aware of the great extent of corruption in our country. But where does it begin? What is its significance in politics and the economy? What threat does it pose to society? Neither sociologists nor economists nor political analysts have devised any theoretical explanation of corruption, any way to interpret it, other than as a chain of criminal acts. No one presents it as something intrinsically woven into the era of socialism.

To this day, only from attorneys and investigators can we learn all the details of the famous Uzbek Cotton Affair, even though the public ought to know about its multifarious aspects, involving, if you add up all the bribes paid out, many millions of rubles. But the testimonies of law-enforcement officials are one-sided: An investigator is primarily interested in the facts of a crime—was a bribe given, and if so, by and to whom, when, and where, in what form, and how much? And the larger the bribe, the more serious the incident, the crime. But the phenomenon the incident represents is actually better understood when the whole web of circumstances is brought to light, when attention is paid even to tiny, barely perceptible details.

The evidence collected in this case—the gold treasures, the diamonds, the gallon jars with coins from the days of the tsars, and the milk pails filled with Soviet bills—is the kind of material evidence upon which investigators and the press love to dwell. But nothing attracts the public's attention like a record of more ordinary booty. Here is an excerpt from Telman Gdlyan's published account of his investigation:

"In November and December, Dustov, at his home in Bukhara, received the following from the First Secretary of the Gizhduvan District Party Committee of Uzbekistan as a bribe: 20,000 rubles, a men's leather jacket valued at 500 rubles, a men's coat valued at 200 rubles, an imported tape recorder valued at 1,500 rubles, and a box of Turkish delights valued at 10 rubles. . . .

"At roughly the same time, in the summer of 1981, I needed some construction materials to build a home in Shakhrisabze. I appealed to Rustamov, who fulfilled my request and gave me three cubic yards of boards and beams. . . . In the same way in mid-1982, Rustamov gave me a boiler, radiators, and pipes for the heating system. . . .

"The chairman of the board of the Bukhara Oblast Consumer Union, Gani Mirazabayev (who had complained to one of the journalists that Karimov, first secretary of the oblast Party committee, had turned him into 'his own personal servant') bought a dozen hot cakes at a neighborhood bakery each morning, and had his chauffeur rush them to his lord highness. It was trivial, of course. But for the hot cakes alone, more than 10,000 rubles had been spent during those years.

"The list of various 'packages' for Dustov consists of almost thirty items, among which are ten pairs of imported socks for the sum of 14 rubles; ten embroidered bathrobes for a total of 2,500 rubles. Together, they made up a total of tens of thousands."[14]

All of these were bribes, but bribes of a special kind. None of them was particularly noteworthy. Ordinary life! Who doesn't know that for any good in short supply (and what isn't?) and for any service, you always have to pay above the established price? What Soviet citizen has not paid over the amount, hasn't greased the palm of a store clerk, a cashier, a bureaucrat, a policeman, a doctor in a hospital, a professor in the university . . . and anyone else?! No one has ever thought this in any way remarkable. Who hasn't presented the "right" people with a box of candy, three yards of planks, or imported socks. Perhaps a more precise formula for this life was found by the former secretary of the Moldavian Communist Party, Viktor Smirnov, subsequently a high official of the USSR Central Committee. When he was arrested for bribes soon after Usmanov (unlike the unfortunate Usmanov, Smirnov was released without any consequences), he said, "I understood that it was a bribe, but by virtue of the existing circumstances, I treated it like a normal phenomenon."

"By virtue of the existing circumstances," everyone takes and everyone gives. Can it really be considered a crime if a person lives like everyone else? Should a normal life-style be reviewed in a criminal trial? Even once he was in jail, Vakhab Usmanov could not accept that he was the subject of a criminal investigation. He was of course familiar with the penal code, but the living, customary law reigned in real life, not the law on the books or judicial law. What the investigator was calling "bribes" or "falsifications" or "embezzlements" was a normal, everyday, customary economic practice. He had lived like everyone else around him and didn't see himself as particularly guilty.

In prison, he felt as if he had been dragged into some propaganda campaign out of the blue, "the battle against corruption." It was a campaign, he thought, which everyone except himself had been warned about. While others had managed to prepare themselves, making up reports and garnering the favorable indicators,* he had been betrayed and sacrificed. Otherwise, instead of languishing in a jail cell, he would be sitting with others in some presidium, pronouncing irate words condemning bribe-takers—the very words that he now was forced to hear from the investigator and the prosecutor. But who would seriously start claiming that you could live without bribing and fixing the books? No, perhaps you could live, but to remain in the seat of the minister, to fulfill your official duties successfully—no, that was impossible.

The investigation paid far less attention to the motives for criminal acts than to the bribe-taking itself. When the investigators were forced to report it anyway, it would turn out that the most common reason for taking a bribe was the need to *give another bribe* in turn. It seemed that Usmanov, any oblast Party secretary, or any Soviet bureaucrat could not fulfill his official duties without taking; otherwise, he simply wouldn't have anything to give.

A. Karimov, the former first secretary of the Bukhara Oblast Party Committee who was pardoned after being sentenced to death, told the investigators: "Who ever gave would be the one to get resources. The State Planning Department simply decided the fate of an entire oblast the size of the territory of a European state. . . . Even stocks and supplies were impossible to receive in full quantity without giving bribes. . . . There was no one to complain to, because all the leaders of Party and soviet bodies and ministries themselves took bribes of various sizes."[15]

The Soviet economy is a black market of monstrous proportions. Nothing is sold freely, everything is in short supply, but anything can be had if you know to whom to give. Usmanov described how each time he came from Tashkent to Moscow, he, a minister, felt as if he had entered a bazaar: the Ministry of Light Industry and the Ministry of Internal Affairs; the Chief Customs

---

*Production quotas/figures. —TRANS.

Inspection Office and the Chief Supply Office; even—it's horrible to say—the General Staff of the Soviet Army, even the Sports Committee. Where *didn't* they take presents, where *didn't* they hand out bribes, who *didn't* they have to treat at their own expense (that's when you needed funds) to dinner in a restaurant, a picnic, or a sauna.

While we were jailed in Lefortovo Prison, Usmanov told me how he'd been there before, for a completely different reason. In the basement of the prison, there is a luxurious sauna frequented by the local bosses and their friends, where he had taken a steam bath. The sauna is the perfect place for business conversations. It was not at the State Planning Department that the fate of the socialist economy was decided, but in the steam room, in the restaurant, at the vacation dacha.

In Moscow, all the favors cost much less than they did in Central Asia. A pair of gold baubles, for example, presented at the USSR Ministry of Light Industry, to which Usmanov and his ministry directly reported, provided the opportunity to change the planned indicators in his favor, to lower by millions the deduction budgeted for the state's coffers.

We should not think that Usmanov came to Moscow to deceive, grab, or steal, or to personally enrich himself. He was faithful to his professional duty, and a conscientious manager. The way he dealt with officials in Moscow, Tashkent, and elsewhere was no more than the customary way for a manager in the Soviet economy. It wasn't that he was immoral, but because it seemed that things wouldn't work any other way, the very machinery of the socialist economy could not operate. And here, in this inability of the socialist economic system to run without bribes, without the so-called shadow relationships, without the wide, complex system of the black market, is something far more mysterious than all the buried treasures or the mafia's dividing up the loot.

For the three-quarters of a century that the Communists ruled Russia, they did everything to destroy the ordinary human relationships of buying and selling—at least in the production sphere—and replace them entirely with centralized planning and distribution of resources. But the living needs of people, the common sense of society, and the demands of production just did not coincide with the plans and orders of Communist bureaucrats. Therefore, even though it was strictly prohibited, the black market flourished even under the threat of jail and the death penalty; and, in doing so, it preserved market relationships, enabling them profoundly and triumphantly to penetrate the entire system of the socialist economy.

One of the peculiarities of the black market is that, because there is no private property, the merchant sells goods that don't belong to him and the buyer does not become the owner of what he buys. Whether it's cotton or a car, pipes or paper, or land, timber, irrigation systems, farms, or factories, they do not belong to local Party officials or ministers or the chairmen of collective farms. But what does belong to them is full discretionary power over these riches, just as in fact they have power over the people who produce these riches. The power itself to control goods is bought and sold. And the position of authority is the ultimate good on the Soviet black market. The "commodity of power" is the most expensive commodity but the most profitable. Should the selling of posts be understood as corruption, that is, as the disintegration of socialism? Or is this in fact the very essence of socialism itself, and in principle there can be no other kind of socialism?

Communist doctrine and all its ruinous consequences for humankind have been studied in detail by many scholars and writers (from the modest but perspicacious Boris Brutskus, who at the beginning of the 1920s proved that any "non-market" economy was impossible, to the more recent writings of Friedrich von Hayek and Aleksandr Solzhenitsyn). But the mechanism of the black market as the essential phenomenon of socialism remains unstudied to this day, and for that reason, seems exclusively a criminal and mysterious area.

The start of the investigation of the Uzbek Cotton Affair is now linked with the brief rule of Yury Andropov. By the time he took office, it was becoming increasingly evident that power openly had a market value. The first investigations proved this point in documentary fashion: The office of a Party district committee secretary could be bought for 10,000 rubles; the position of chief of the Internal Affairs Administration of an oblast was up for grabs at the bazaar; the opportunity to become director of a sovkhoz was for sale. Quite simply, a black market in power was as common as the black market in goods or official services.

But that was only half the problem. In and of themselves, these facts would not have alarmed the highest Party leaders—after all, they knew only too well that neither Party nor economic management positions were given out for free. True, in the old days, payment for positions of power was made not in actual cash but in a more valuable currency: loyalty to the doctrine and the leadership, unconditional agreement to observe the established rules of Party relations, and, most important, good indicators of overfulfillment of plans and orders. All of these indicators were more important than money. And we suppose that Andropov's distrust was not aroused by the moral character of officials. The whole danger was that power, which previously could not be purchased by anything except loyalty and good indicators, was now selling for money.

One episode from Telman Gdlyan's investigative files vividly illustrates how the fundamental principles of Communist doctrine clash with the pervasive reality of the market.

An oblast-level police chief was interrogated. "I believed my indicators were no worse than in other oblasts, but I understood that the ministry doesn't like any fooling around," he explained to the investigator, and you would have to have a heart of stone not to sympathize with the man. We understand: the indicators are the chief value of the Communist doctrine. What can you do if the boss is not happy with your indicators? Here is what you do:

"I believed my indicators were no worse than in other oblasts, but I understood that the ministry doesn't like any fooling around. I knew that Dustov gave bribes to the minister, and decided through him to give a bribe to Ergashev. I gave Dustov 10,000 rubles and asked him to give it to the minister."[16]

How simple. And who will dare to claim that this incident is the only one of its kind, or that situations of this kind occur just in certain republics or with people of certain nationalities? Let us recall an example from the year 1960. Although this file never reached the stage of criminal investigation, it involved large-scale tampering with production figures in Ryazan oblast, and ended with the suicide of Aleksei Larionov, secretary of the oblast Party committee. How many crimes were there like this in the past, how many are there now and will there continue to be?

If there was nothing unique about fixing numbers, if good socialist indicators can be bought and sold and made a universal standard, then can the reality of socialism be understood by looking only at the "administrative-command" side of the system? How could we not help but see that Soviet reality displayed a paradoxical historical regularity: the power that restricts or even prohibits healthy market relations of buying and selling inevitably becomes, itself, a market commodity and an object of speculation. It is as if the value of everything that is prohibited were transferred to this power. Is this process not the historical essence of our era?

The struggle for power is incorporated in man at a biological level. Even in prison it does not disappear, although one would think there is no way you could wield power over anyone or anything there because, just the opposite, everyone and everything there brutally wields power over you. But it does not disappear—it merely takes on distorted forms. Each morning, Vakhab Usmanov took out of his nightstand a red cardboard folder which the investigator had given him. Seating himself at this little stand, which served as a table, he wrote out his confessions. Day after day, he recalled the people who had given him bribes, and the people whom he himself had bribed.

All of them were people in power, people who still lived freely and did not realize that their fate now depended on a man writing into a red folder in his jail cell in Lefortovo. All of them were now in his power. Later, when I was somewhere in transit (or perhaps already in labor camp), a rumor caught up with me about the people prosecuted along with Usmanov. Altogether, he had brought about 400 people down with him. Recalling the red folder, I believed it.

For many years, the Uzbek Party and economic leaders reported inflated indicators to the central authorities. They would add millions of tons to the actual amount of raw cotton turned over to the government. The money received for the nonexistent cotton was embezzled. These stolen billions finally ended up being injected into shadowy black-market dealings, including the purchase and sale of official positions, which fostered universal corruption in the republic. It was a well-known criminal formula.

We already have an idea of what a criminal looks like—here he is in a jail cell writing down his confessions and putting them into a red folder. But what does the person he stole from look like? That's what really amazes us. How could you go on for five years—a minimum of five years!—and not notice that you are being robbed of billions?

The stories of how the Uzbek investigations began—with the accidental exposure of a 40,000-ruble bribe, brought to Moscow to some textile factory instead of cotton—are tales for the naïve. How is it that you could notice only accidentally that 2 billion rubles in cash were stolen? How could you not see that in your accounting, one thing is written on paper, but in reality 4 million tons are missing? That amount of *anything* would be hard to miss.

You could overlook such a thing for only one reason: if there was nothing to notice, if you received exactly as much of a commodity as you had paid for. If there was nothing missing, if there were no shortages, if there was no inflated number, and everything was in place.

I do not know if any economists were brought into the Uzbek Cotton Affair, but if they were, they could not help but see that this case is a most interesting example of price formation in practice. If you forget completely about the existence of the indicators and began to count only money and tons of cotton, then the arithmetic is quite simple, even for an elementary school student: the buyer (the state) annually acquires 5 million tons of cotton, but pays for 6 million tons. The result is that the actual cotton turns out to be one sixth more expensive than was supposed.

In this light, all conversations about inflated indicators or about money not backed by goods become pointless.

For five years the Soviet economy quietly reconciled itself to a 20 percent increase in the price of cotton. Nothing collapsed as a result (at least not back then)—the cotton mills didn't grind to a halt, the fabric presses didn't shut down, and the garment factories weren't empty. That means, from an economic point of view, the cotton price set by the Uzbek swindlers was an intelligent one. If it was not quite the price of balance between supply and demand, then it was close to it. The buyer was prepared to pay such a price, could pay it, and did pay it.

It is helpful to know that the nominal wholesale cost of Uzbek cotton in recent years has been roughly five to ten times lower than world prices even if we use the official exchange rate. The difference is therefore so great that it is as if we were talking about different historical eras rather than different countries.

The standard of living in Uzbek villages also belongs to another civilization. The average wage of cotton pickers is less than 150 rubles per month. Even when the ruble was worth at least something, this was below poverty level.

The republicwide poverty in Uzbekistan is the main reason not only for the social, but for the well-known environmental, disaster of this region. In the drive for the planned indicators of the socialist system, pesticides and other poisonous chemicals were used without restriction, so that now in some provinces of the republic two out of every three young nursing mothers have been found to have unacceptably high levels of toxins in their breast milk. The infant mortality rate in Uzbekistan is similar to that found in African countries with high numbers of AIDS cases. Meanwhile, there is no way of stopping the use of defoliants and other harmful chemicals, and no way to neutralize them; Uzbekistan has no money for clean-up.

In our country, cotton has always been cheap, not because there was a lot of it on the market or because it was easily produced (no, there is no market as such, and the cheapness of cotton is artificial), but because the price was deliberately kept low. (In fact, prices are kept low on other types of agricultural products as well, such as grain, potatoes, and meat.) The very structure of the price of cotton does not include the full cost of labor or the full cost of the use of natural resources. Thus, from the outset, both the poverty of the peasant and the ecological catastrophes are programmed into the economy.

In addition, pricing is the most important instrument of power. Setting prices is the privilege and right of the bureaucrats of the ruling apparat. Or rather, it is not just a privilege and a right, but a kind of fundamental, sacred principle of Communist doctrine. And it was for violating this sacred principle by letting the market establish prices that Vakhab Usmanov and his co-defendants faced charges (and they themselves have little understanding of why they faced charges).

But to return to the Uzbek Cotton Affair itself. For the sake of convenience, we have substituted our own terms for the standard terms—instead of talking about the inflation of socialist indicators, we've spoken about the rise in the cost of cotton, as in a market economy. But embezzlement is theft no matter what you call it. Who pocketed the billions received as a result of this improvised price increase? The personal consumption of even the 30,000 people sentenced under the Uzbek Cotton Affair and their families can account for only several tens of millions. Where is the rest of the money? Not a penny of it fell to the cotton pickers, whose monthly wages don't reach 150 rubles. Even if the cotton were purchased strictly at the actual market price, the Uzbek peasants would not get a ruble more than they do now.

Somehow, the embezzled money disappeared outright. Or at least its previous form and economic essence were changed beyond recognition through a deal whereby money was paid to fictitious offices for nonexistent cotton. Thus this money was removed from planned socialist circulation forever, and thrown into the sea of spontaneous economic relations. From non-cash funds,* circulating in the socialist world like phantoms, where there exist planned and reported indicators, these millions turned into cash that could be tendered in the world of living supply and demand. In other words, this money entered the black market.

After all, the special feature of the black market is not so much the material valuables that circulate as the power to *allocate* these valuables. On the black market, the actual rubles do not purchase an automobile, a tractor, or a steam engine but only the *right* to come to a distributor's organization and arrange the purchase of the good from the state. We pay the cash to the person who has the power to allocate the item we need. Furthermore, that person will still turn over the planned, cashless amounts to the state coffers. But you pay in cash for the very opportunity to make a purchase.

Is this a bribe? Yes, it is a bribe. But a bribe, among other definitions, in our situation is also a special instrument for balancing price in accordance with supply and demand. It is an instrument through which an additional permission fee is brought into the price, a fee permitting the circumvention of existing restrictions. Obviously, these regulations are always a source of quick profit for whoever has the power to arbitrarily impose or slacken them (and a source of loss for whoever has to go around them). Communist economic regulations have always cost the people and society dearly. They continue to do so, but now more and more expenses are paid in cash—in real black-market money. Increasingly, permission can be bought—in the direct meaning of the word.

Today, thank God, black-market deals have begun to be noted by lawyers, journalists, and professional economists. For example, in the so-called 500 Days program, 146 billion rubles were included as black-market profits. But the black market continues to be understood only as something criminal, as a shadow sphere

---

*A type of credit allocated by the government and also used between enterprises in socialist accounting. —TRANS.

counterpoising the legal economy controlled by the ruling apparat. And for that reason, the true and comprehensive role of the black market in the life of our country continues to slip by the attention of the specialists. Somehow, we must not miss the real point of the most important changes occurring in the country.

The Uzbek Cotton Affair reveals for all to see the general practice—the logically and historically inevitable practice—of buying and selling official positions and favors. Power itself has become a commodity—and its price is rising. Socialist indicators have now been pushed aside by the cash nexus and other market values. With historical inevitability Communist doctrine is turning the country into a grand black market and the ruling apparat into a criminal mafia.

A person in prison is left only with what God has given him: intellect, kindness, love, despair, anger. Everything that comes from other people—career, honor, wealth—disappears. As I gazed at Usmanov, it was difficult to imagine how this miserable, bewildered child, begging for a morsel of hope from us, his cellmates, could ever have been the powerful lord of a large industrial sector, with factories, receiving stations, thousands of workers. In the cell, he was pathetic in the literal meaning of the word—he aroused pity. For example, he could not even clip his own nails. After getting some scissors from the warden, he puzzled over them for a while, as if trying to remember how to use them. He managed to cut the nails on his left hand, but for his right hand he had to call on our third cellmate, a university professor who had been jailed for some shady dealings with foreign students. Usmanov clearly took pleasure in the manicure; he smiled, and spoke some affectionate words in Uzbek, explaining to us that at home his wife cut his nails. The professor became irritated and demanded that his client stop squirming.

The longer the investigation continued, the more difficult it became for Usmanov to retain a sense of his own importance, of his membership in the highest, most select echelon of society. His sense of position would alternately wax and wane, depending on the rank of the investigator interrogating him at the time. When it was the Deputy Prosecutor General who came to question him about the nature of his dealings with the Party leadership, he would return to the cell animated and in a better mood, as if he had once again been put on his Party rations. On the other hand, after interrogation by lieutenants from the provincial prosecutor's office involving explanations of petty details, Usmanov would return to the cell depressed. Refusing to play chess, he would flop down on his cot, turn his face to the wall, and lie in that position for hours. Sometimes he would even remember that his grandfather had been a cleric, and he would begin to pray, loudly calling upon Allah.

Meanwhile, the investigation zigged and zagged. Judging from what Usmanov told us, all the circumstances of the crimes in question had been brought to light, all the details uncovered. Even so, it was not in the least clear what final summation should be drawn from them. And in the nature of Soviet judicial practice, no trial could take place without such a final summation, provided by the appropriate Party office. In such major cases of great state import, a trial took place in order to properly establish the opinion of the Party leadership and translate it into a court judgment. Thus, everyone was anticipating that a decision by someone or other would be coming down any moment.

All the major Uzbek cases were brought by the KGB. The highly centralized KGB structure lay almost completely outside the control of local Party bodies. Thus, the decision to launch the investigation necessarily emanated from the top and would have come directly from Andropov himself. But Andropov did not clearly see "the essence of processes occurring, their sources, and causal connections," as Party journalists love to put it.[17] Otherwise he would have given the investigation a completely different, more restricted focus. In fact, in instigating the case, he would seem to have sincerely assumed that this was a matter of a corrupted elite of a republic Party leadership. He believed it was within his rights to make the most rigorous demands of his subordinates, or to remove them altogether and replace them with others. It did not seem at all terrible to him if some connections were exposed between corrupt elements in Tashkent and in Moscow. The purge would then be all the more justified. The former KGB chief conceived of himself as a noble gardener, called on to weed out the Party garden entrusted to him.

In reality, everything turned out to be much more complicated. Andropov was mistaken in thinking that he was beginning an internal Party investigation. Gorbachev, forced to continue his predecessor's hastily conceived effort, already possessed the materials of the case and could not help but understand (and perhaps he had always understood, even before any Uzbek investigation) that by his very position as General Secretary he, too, and all previous leaders were not gardeners, but the central figures of the many divergent criminal structures—their chiefs, leaders, *pakhany,* and "godfathers." No matter how strong their personal power, they could not change anything in these structures. The criminal essence of Communist doctrine and of the General Secretary's power was revealed in the Uzbek affairs—openly, and stripped of ideological covering. The Party had turned into a mafia.

In this situation the best thing that Gorbachev could do was to take the information for his own knowledge and quickly close the case, designating it as a local matter (which it should have been from the outset). The irresponsible proposals of other politicians to investigate the matter to the end only irritated him. For instance, Yeltsin toured Uzbekistan while a Central Committee secretary and reported on the corruption upon his return: "Suddenly, Gorbachev became angry, saying that I didn't understand anything at all, and that Usmankhodzhayev was an honest Communist, and that he had simply been forced to fight against Rashidovism, and the old mafia was vilifying him with false denunciations and slander."[18]*

---

*Inamzhon Usmankhodzhayev was one of the defendants in the Uzbek Cotton Affair, accused of giving bribes to Politburo member Yegor Ligachev. He later retracted his testimony, claiming it had been extracted under threats from the prosecutors, and apologized to Ligachev. Sharaf Rashidov, the Uzbek Communist leader under Brezhnev, had also been accused of corruption. —TRANS.

Thus Gorbachev provided the formula which was supposed to be used in the review of the Uzbek cases: the "old mafia" were those criminal structures that had been publicly exposed, and the "honest Communists" were all of those whom the mafia opposed. The entire affair is thereby translated from the sphere of economics and politics to the sphere of morals and linguistic constructions. For specialists in propaganda, all the rest was just a matter of technique. The "honest Communists" immediately and simply overcame the "old mafia"—we can read about this in an article by the same Usman-khodzhayev, first secretary of the Uzbekistan Communist Party, published a year after Usmanov's death sentence:

"At the Twenty-seventh Communist Party Congress, the January [1987] Central Committee Plenum, the activity of the Uzbekistan Communist Party was subjected to harsh but just criticism. A particularly harsh, unpleasant evaluation was given to the *distortion of Leninist principles of selection, appointment, and training of cadres* that had been tolerated in the recent past [emphasis added]."[19] The article also noted that since 1984, 90.4 percent of the cadres of the USSR Communist Party Central Committee *nomenklatura* had been replaced, as were 76.6 percent of the *nomenklatura* of the Uzbekistan Communist Party Central Committee. The "old mafia," we suppose, was replaced by the "honest Communists."

The cadres were to blame. The old mafia. The criminal clan. Scoundrels who had wormed their way into the Party. Nine-tenths of the cadres of the Central Committee *nomenklatura* can be sacrificed, if only it will keep away the threat from the doctrine itself, if only it will instill in public consciousness the authorities' verbal formulas. Paradoxically, this was helped along by the campaign launched by Telman Gdlyan and Nikolai Ivanov and later supported by Tatyana Koryagina. Their attacks on the Kremlin leadership and their hints at corruption among individual high-ranking leaders, right up to Gorbachev, actually made it possible to narrow the dimensions of the case in the public mind. Instead of focusing on the system and its rulers, everyone's gaze fell on individuals. It must be the "bad people" in the apparat. Soon public attention was concentrated on whether Viktor Smirnov was guilty, and to what extent. Should they go after Smirnov, or not?

The very translation of the affair into strictly legal and moral terms was an enormous tactical victory for the apparat. Here, as in the first stages of the investigation, the most powerful force at the Communists' disposal was brought in—the KGB. But if during the first phases, the KGB was supposed to give the case the inertia of motion, now its task was the reverse—to quell that inertia. Manipulating the attention of the public, creating certain public expectations, and changing them from trial to trial was not at all hard to do. Usmanov was to be executed; A. Karimov was to be sentenced to death but then pardoned; Yury Churbanov, the son-in-law of Leonid Brezhnev, was also to be caught in the Uzbek extortions, but given a ridiculously light sentence; Khaydar Yakhyayev (Minister of Internal Affairs) and Usmankhodzhayev were to be held in prison and then freed; a noisy fuss was to be whipped up around Smirnov, but in the end he was to be released.

Usmanov was the victim of this subtle policy. His execution was the necessary dot that had to be placed above the "i" in any event. Too much hatred had accumulated in society against the ruling apparat, and therefore someone had to be demonstratively shot. Society had to be shown indicators of justice in action, and the earlier, the better. It was best that someone at a fairly high level be sacrificed—but in the economic, not the Party, hierarchy. Surely it was clear that you wouldn't take out and shoot Churbanov, a member of the General Secretary's family. When people were outraged at the light sentence Churbanov received, the judges justified it by saying that they had executed Usmanov—what else did people want? Vladimir I. Terebilov, then chairman of the USSR Supreme Court, spoke of passions lingering around the so-called Churbanov Affair in an interview:

"In my view, these passions are being artificially maintained by persons with vested interests. The case was heard by experienced judges and people's assessors. Until now, there has been no protest from the prosecutor general about the case.* Perhaps it should be noted that in addition to the case mentioned, two other criminal cases concerning the Uzbek SSR were heard at the USSR Supreme Court. The chief accused were the former Minister of the Cotton-Refining Industry, Usmanov, and the former First Secretary of the Bukhara Oblast Party Committee, Karimov, who were sentenced to the highest measure of punishment;† Churbanov and a number of other officials were sentenced to lengthy terms of imprisonment; only one accused was acquitted."[20]

That's it! What else do you need? Usmanov was executed by firing squad. The doctrine remained alive. It stood vindicated. Or, to be more precise, the crimes that it was responsible for were not even investigated.

As before, the country remained under the power of the Communists. The tactic of such investigations was still determined by the KGB. But as it turns out, not for long. The time has come when a detailed study or investigation has begun of the real embodiment of the state doctrine of the Communists.

*Postscript:* In December 1991, as this book was being finished, the newspapers reported that all those who had previously been tried in the Uzbek corruption cases had been released. Then why was Usmanov executed?

---

*In the Soviet system, the prosecutor general can call for the reopening of a case if he has grounds to believe there was a mistrial. —TRANS.

†The Soviet term for the death penalty. —TRANS.

# CHAPTER SEVEN

*Witness Testimony*

# Konstantin Maydanyuk,
# Senior Special Cases Investigator

*Until recently, Konstantin Maydanyuk was one of the best-known investigators in the country. The USSR Prosecutor's Office appointed him to investigate the notorious corruption cases of the highest Party and economic apparatchiks, including the Uzbek Cotton Affair. He did his job capably, and a brilliant career awaited him. But in 1988 he resigned from the prosecutor's office suddenly and vanished from the public eye. He changed his place of work several times afterward within a short period, as if he were hiding from persecution.*

*I finally tracked him down. I knew that he had investigated the case of Vakhab Usmanov and had opposed the death sentence. Unfortunately, nobody paid attention to his opinion.*

LEV TIMOFEYEV: Did you leave the investigator's office because you were afraid you'd be killed? Were you threatened?

KONSTANTIN MAYDANYUK: There were no threats like that and no fears, but there were many other reasons. I worked for six years in the USSR Prosecutor's Office and covered the cases that were out of the ordinary: the Krasnodar Affair, where the whole state and Party system was involved; Uzbekistan—all those cases in the Cotton Affair; then Baku; then here in Moscow, with the abuses in the Ministry of Culture. These criminal cases enabled me to see the entire system of relations in our society and state. It was one thing to view all of these things from the outside and another to penetrate within.

LT: How exactly did you regard your own role in this system, so that you quit your work as an investigator?

KM: I realized that I was a part of this system. All of us were all parts of this system. And if you speak of the mental and moral side, I was especially interested in the point of view of those who say that they sincerely believe in the ideas of the Communists. I think that they were the most outrageous hypocrites. I think that in this system, there can't be a single person who would sincerely believe—it was all so obviously pointless. Everyone understood everything, but I don't know people in my world who would have followed the call of Solzhenitsyn not to live by the lie. At least not to participate. I did not want to participate, so I left.

LT: All right, let us look at the case not as participants, but from the outside. As far as I know, you were not involved in probing political cases, but in the process of the investigation, you could not have helped but come across connections between your subjects of inquiry and the political structures. How far up the ladder of power did these connections go?

KM: That type of investigation became possible only in recent times—starting about 1978. Then, as more and more major figures began to appear in the cases, there were greater opportunities for investigation, and the degree of what was permitted increased. At first it was on a low level—that of district Party committees, city Party committees. And then my target became the secretary of the Krasnodar Territory Party Committee. His name was Anatoly Georgievich Tarada.

LT: Who died later, apparently?

KM: He died in a prison cell from a stroke.

LT: There was some doubt as to whether he had died of natural causes.                                                          •

KM: That's just a doubt; I don't have any facts. He died after an interrogation in which he had given serious testimony regarding Central Committee workers. He died that same night.

LT: And then, naturally, his testimonies had no value after that?

KM: They didn't go any further, because testimonies alone are very little to go on. Only a certain amount of evidence is needed to apprehend a person who has committed an ordinary theft, but in order to arrest a deputy minister you need something else; all questions have to be decided at the level of the Central Committee and the Party Control Commission.

LT: How high were the positions of the people against whom Tarada had testified?

KM: Very high. At the level of department heads of the Central Committee. These were very big figures for those times.

LT: Was it a question of corruption?

KM: Yes.

LT: Now some of these apparatchiks seem to be going quietly into oblivion or into murky, semicriminal structures. Some of them have done just the opposite: they've broken loudly with the Party, announced their exit, and crossed over to the democrats' camp. People say that the corrupt apparatchiks have gone into the mafia structures, and people with a clean conscience have turned to the democrats. Is that the case?

KM: Honest—dishonest; good—bad. I will dare to make the claim that you do not have to spend a long time figuring out whether a person receives bribes if he works in the administration of material and technical supply, for example. He receives a miserable wage. Besides his desk and chair, he has nothing. He knows that in other ministries people of lower rank than himself make big money. The system is closed, and you don't see where the beginning is. Therefore in order to get goods from this official, you have to give him a bribe.

If I gave a bribe in Moscow to procure some goods and came back home to Tashkent, where I have the power to allocate those goods, then as a minimum, I have to reimburse myself for these expenses I had in Moscow. But I can't simply reimburse my expenses, otherwise what's the point of all the trouble I've gone to? If I get 1,000 automobiles, for example, I take something for what I paid in Moscow plus I receive a certain amount more so that my own activity is profitable. And that's the way it is absolutely everywhere. If you leave one job, you go to another place where exactly the same principle operates. Where can you go? Can you leave here? Or can you leave this life (as some have done when they received their first warrants for interrogations)? You talk about honest or dishonest, democrats or conservatives. The people this system produces bring their habits with them. They haven't become different. So I'm very skeptical about what's going on in the country now.

LT: But Gorbachev? And Yeltsin? And the leaders of the Central Asian republics?

KM: Well, are they exceptions of some kind? They are people of the same system. They grew up in it. They don't hide that.

LT: But we are talking about economic relations, or actually—what is more interesting—whether or not these connections have been maintained in the area of political relations; and whether they influence political decisions; and if so, in what way?

KM: I don't get involved in politics. Furthermore, knowing what goes on from the newspapers, from the very beginning I haven't felt optimistic.

LT: Why are you pessimistic?

KM: Essentially, power remains in the very same hands. Power, the economy, and distribution.

LT: Does that mean that the criminal structures have also survived these changes?

KM: I'm now involved in entrepreneurship—or, to put it more precisely, I'm trying to get involved. I come into contact with that world I used to fight against—not with specific people, but with the social milieu. I have the opportunity to witness the same processes from the inside. Former bureaucrats, those who used to run the administrative economic system, have poured into this milieu. They instantly used their connections, spreading metastases in this new fabric. They do everything in order to come more closely and definitively to property. Before, they possessed it indirectly, but now they have the opportunity to possess it directly. With the help of intermediaries, they are creating commercial enterprises and gaining ownership of property. Meanwhile they preserve their places in the structure of power. An intensive process of privatization without official announcement is under way. Everyone knows how this is being done.

LT: So does that mean that you are a mafioso yourself now?

KM: I had to start from zero. In the classic sense of the word, no, I'm not. But in our country now, any professional corporation can, strictly speaking, be called a mafia. People talk about mafiosi in the central directorate, mafiosi in the barbershop; even the guy who collects your garbage is a mafioso. I belong to a corporation of commodities traders. In that sense, I am a mafioso.

# CHAPTER EIGHT

# The Party in the Perestroika Period:
# The President in a Glass Bowl

Mikhail Gorbachev was sent into retirement with honor and respect. He was called the father of perestroika and the democratic
transformations that followed. He was truly unlike his Communist
predecessors. Even before he became General Secretary, during his
first visit to England, he shocked Western observers:

"When Gorbachev came to Chequers for lunch, [Margaret]
Thatcher came out to meet him at the entrance. 'From the very first
second he made a very strong impression,' an aide who was
present recalled. 'A sense of force and energy radiated from him,
as from a coiled spring. He smiled readily, his face was mobile, not
gloomy and stern, like some Gromyko. He knew how to crack a
joke.' "[21]

The British didn't yet realize (nor did we in Russia) that this man
was a great reformer. By then he had already formed the opinion
that "everything was rotten" in the Soviet Communist system.
What is more, he had already discussed this with close friends in
the Party (Eduard Shevardnadze, for example), and they agreed
with him.

Is Gorbachev really the father of perestroika? We aren't children,
after all, believing that the greatest event of the twentieth century—the fall of the Communist regime—happened because Gorbachev, unlike Gromyko, smiled readily and could crack a joke, or
because he and Shevardnadze, like some Marcellus and Horatio of

our day, had agreed that everything was rotten in the state of the USSR. Chernenko certainly didn't think that anything was rotten. So in what way was Gorbachev better in Chernenko's eyes (and Gromyko's and Ustinov's) than, say, Grishin or Romanov, from whom as much of a sense of energy radiated? Finally let us recall how much energy Khrushchev had, and what a knack for telling a joke: but in 1964 he failed to serve someone's interests and was crudely removed. Isn't it better to try to understand what forces pushed Gorbachev forward, or, to be more precise, pushed him into the General Secretary's seat? Whose interests did he serve, or was he obliged to serve? Whose perception of what had to be done did he coincide with?

One of the leading perestroika figures, the writer and poet Vitaly Korotich, once editor-in-chief of the journal *Ogonyok*, believes that throughout Gorbachev's reign he was never free to make his own decisions and always depended on some secret structures. "We will not know the true level of his dependency for some time to come," said Korotich in the fall of 1991, as he prepared to leave for the United States to teach. (Many people in Russia saw Korotich's departure as a retreat or even a flight under the pressure of direct threats of physical harm that had been made by political opponents. In speaking of Gorbachev's dependence, Korotich was seeking to explain his own exhaustion, his despair and pessimism, which apparently were driving him out of the country.)

Korotich's statements carry great weight. We will recall that the most sensational exposés of the party mafia in Uzbekistan were published in 1987 in his journal. In the summer of 1988, Korotich addressed the Nineteenth All-Union Party Conference; his sensational statement that some of the *nomenklatura* apparatchiks present at that august meeting were criminals, bribe-takers, and embezzlers had a powerful political effect. He named no names, but the whole country, following the conference on television, tried to guess whom he meant. Any of the Party figures sitting in the hall could be suspected of bribe-taking and embezzlement. In a way, Korotich was pushing Gorbachev into fighting with the elite of the

Party apparat. Public opinion was being prepared for a change of Party leadership, and in fact, soon all of them were removed from their posts for various reasons.

During the Gorbachev years, *Ogonyok,* along with several other publications (*Moscow News, Argumenty i fakty,* and later, *Komsomolskaya pravda*) waged a steady propaganda campaign in favor of democratic reforms. The editorial boards supported Gorbachev's policies, believed in Gorbachev, and defended Gorbachev from attacks "from the right." Therefore, it was all the more strange when Gorbachev himself, somehow overlooking this support, attacked democratic publications in general and *Ogonyok* in particular.

Once Gorbachev called Korotich into his office and staged a temper tantrum, as if to dissociate himself from the political position of this democratic editor. For his part, Korotich believes that such loud, hysterical tantrums were meant more for the walls (which he thinks had eyes and ears) than for himself. "I'm convinced he was bugged. And that he knew it," he said. "When he yelled at me, it was not like him at all. There was something incomprehensible about it. 'Ligachev has been on the Central Committee for seventeen years, and I trust him,' ranted Mikhail Sergeyevich. 'What, are you trying to tell me who my friends and enemies are?' he asked, his voice breaking into a scream, but with his eyes completely calm and benign. And I choked on the boiled sausage sandwich he had served me, and didn't understand a thing. Gorbachev staged similar performances several times, intended for the hidden eyes and ears. It was no wonder Yakovlev merely grinned during this display of pseudo-hysterics."[22]

Whose eyes and ears could be in the office of the President of the largest country in the world? On whom was the General Secretary of the ruling Party dependent? What was Yakovlev grinning at, exactly? These answers are not given, but it is as if it is understood that everyone knows them. It was true that Korotich's bitter exposés did not become a sensation. They merely confirmed the prevailing opinion that Gorbachev was not what he seemed. Because he understood his dependent position, distanced himself from the democratic wing, he deliberately demonstrated his distance, and he was afraid of fighting with the Party apparat (or the mafia, the clan, or some other criminal structure merely covering for that apparat).

In fact, many people had noted that, in contrast to the abruptness and at times outright rudeness he displayed toward the democrats (for instance, his slighting of Academician Sakharov when he was chairing the Congress of People's Deputies), Gorbachev unfailingly maintained a silent tolerance of figures who advocated retaining the Empire and the Party, like the conservative parliamentary caucus known as Soyuz, or Union, although they attacked the President openly and often rudely.

Vitaly Korotich was correct: the secret authorities who actually directed policy always kept Gorbachev in a glass bowl. He was continually surrounded by a tight ring of hostile agents. Here, for example, is a typical agent's report to KGB chief Vladimir Kryuchkov:

"According to information from those close to M. S. Gorbachev, in the next two or three days he must make decisions that will crucially influence further developments in the USSR and affect the final choice of fundamental direction in domestic and foreign policy. These decisions relate to measures taken recently by Prime Minister Valentin Pavlov and the Cabinet of Ministers.

". . . Do not drive Gorbachev into a corner, but try to find a middle ground between him and Pavlov and the groups and forces supporting the Prime Minister. In particular, according to the source, it would be expedient to create a situation whereby Gorbachev would virtually concede to Pavlov's line while simultaneously offering him the opportunity to correct publicly some of the elements of his program and political line.

"According to the source, those close to Gorbachev believe that the most influential figure who could coordinate such tactics with the President would be Kryuchkov."[23]

Obviously, the agents planted among those close to Gorbachev did not limit themselves to the passive transmission of information to the KGB. They also had the active assignment of shaping the

President's views and creating slanted perceptions about the state of affairs in the country.

Gorbachev's dependency became even more obvious in the fall of 1990, when the President betrayed the agreement he had reached with Russian leader Boris Yeltsin about the beginning of radical economic reforms under the 500 Days program. Once again, this time in a manner that removed all doubt, he demonstrated that he was first and foremost a "man of the apparat."

The 500 Days program was drafted by a group of liberal economists led initially by Grigory Yavlinsky and then by Stanislav Shatalin. The program envisioned the liberalization of the economy based on the restoration to the people of the right to private property abolished by the Communists in 1918. If the program had been carried out, the enormous black market, flourishing under the sponsorship of the Communists until the end of 1990, would have ceased to exist. The open market, private initiative, and private enterprise would have taken their place.

The parliament, or Supreme Soviet, of the RSFSR approved the program. It simultaneously passed a law that acknowledged in legislation—for the first time since 1918, although with reservations—the right to own land as private property. If the program had been approved by Gorbachev and the USSR Supreme Soviet, the country would have entered an era of free economics, and quite possibly avoided the profound economic and political crisis of the 1990s.

The 500 Days program specifically defined privatization as the main direction for the immediate start of economic reform. Such reform would end Communist economic methods and the Party apparat's monopoly on the disposition of all material, cultural, and spiritual treasures of the country.

Naturally, this program caused panic and fierce bureaucratic opposition in the Party apparat structures. Nevertheless, in August 1990, Gorbachev and Yeltsin came to an agreement that such reform was necessary.

The two leaders' agreement instilled confidence that the country was finally on the road to liberal transformations. In October, however, everything changed: even though Gorbachev had approved 500 Days, the USSR Supreme Soviet, more obedient to the Party apparat than its Russian counterpart (there were many Party functionaries of various ranks within it), passed a completely different economic program, proposed by then–Prime Minister Nikolai Ryzhkov.

The Ryzhkov plan proposed a catastrophically slow pace of change. The economic structure stayed essentially the same as it had been since the Stalin years. Although a "pluralism of property" was formally included in the program, only weak measures of quasi-privatization were provided; as a result, the economy remained completely under the control of the ruling apparat. Furthermore, despite a virtual ban on private property and private initiative, a swift price hike was planned. Such a price hike could produce rapid impoverishment, provoking widespread unrest. A harsh regime with the Party apparat in power might then be justified as a means to stop the disorders. (The intent of this secret strategy was revealed by the August 1991 coup.)

With the failure of 500 Days, the opponents of reform had triumphed. Now it seemed finally clear whose man Gorbachev was. In a speech before Party members, Ivan Polozkov, leader of the Russian Communist Party and an advocate of preserving the apparat's power, confirmed that it was recommended to President (and General Secretary) Gorbachev at a Politburo session that he choose another program "to somewhat correct the direction" instead of 500 Days.[24]

Shortly afterward, in the middle of February 1991, Yury Prokofyev, First Secretary of the Moscow City Party Committee, also confirmed that at night sessions of the Politburo, Gorbachev was forced to reject the Shatalin-Yavlinsky program. After the President's speech at a session of the USSR Supreme Soviet in December 1990 (when several deputies including Col. Viktor Alksnis, the leader of Soyuz, called for his resignation), once again at a night session of the Politburo, members suggested to Gorbachev the adoption of a new, more hard-line program.[25]

Of course, it is hardly likely that the sessions really were held at night. But the information in the democratic press about them was not rebutted officially. Even if the time of day was incorrect, the public perception of the highest Party gatherings as conspiratorial and mafia-like in nature, and of the President as so dependent on this mafia that he could be taken and "worked over" at any time of the day, was still faithfully conveyed.

The Party apparat was constantly moving toward conspiracy, even somewhat dramatically, as if there were some unceasing war game with a demonstration of mystery, a game intended merely for the viewer, for outward effect.

The Central Committee was perpetually on a war footing. The structures of its apparat were located in the very center of Moscow for the whole country to see but were kept thoroughly secret. Budget, sources of income, and expense items were top secret. Some of the Central Committee's resolutions were stamped "top secret" and distributed only to a restricted list of the highest officials. Documents passed back and forth between the top Party offices by specially armed military couriers. The list of numbers in the special telephone system serving the Central Committee leadership was kept confidential, given only to others on the list upon signature (whenever an updated list was published, the previous one was destroyed).

Former officers of the Party staff say that there were three degrees of secrecy—"special file," which was the strictest; then "top secret," and finally simply "secret." The "secret" stamp was used on documents that contained no information on Party or state secrets but displayed the work methods of Party committees.

But no matter how dramatically the Party apparat displayed its secret might, in reality, the Politburo's indisputable influence on the President in the 500 Days program seems strange. Several months earlier, at the Twenty-eighth Party Congress, at Gorbachev's own initiative the top body of the Party was reorganized. Ligachev, Yakovlev, and Shevardnadze were replaced by unknowns, by faceless and utterly insignificant people. So whose opinion was so seriously significant for the country and the President? Whom did he heed and obey? Was it really the conservatives Prokofyev and Polozkov, characters out of a political lampoon?

It is exactly this lack of correlation between the insignificant Politburo and the suddenly obedient Gorbachev that compels us to posit the existence of another, hidden mechanism for making the most important political decisions. In such a mechanism, the Politburo is only a superficial part, put forward deliberately for show. Such a supposition seems all the more reasonable when we recall that the declining, corrupted Party apparat was largely dependent by that time on the KGB and the military-industrial complex as well as on the shadow enterprises and outright criminal structures.

Whatever the case, the unmotivated and inexplicable turnaround in Gorbachev's political orientation late in 1990 put an end to economic reform, setting the stage for growing economic and public disorganization and chaos. What kind of processes were under way to resist all kinds of economic reform? To whom was Gorbachev being so obliging? Whom was he serving, and upon whom did he depend—the conservatives, the democrats, or some third power?

In order to understand whose side Gorbachev was on—or more precisely, to whom he had to answer—we must examine how the Communist Party split. Who were the Party "conservatives" and who were the "reformers"?

For the advocates of a conservative line, the old Party structures were synonymous with power. These were people of middling or somewhat higher-than-middling ranks of the Party apparat, but not the highest—no higher than the level of the secretaries of the oblast committees. They had been nominated to the Politburo only recently. They might suspect the presence of secret structures and connections, but they were not necessarily completely informed (even as they fulfilled the will of those secret structures). They had grasped once and forever that the perks they enjoyed— the money, the privileges, and the right to distribute enormous material wealth—were given along with the position in the ruling apparat. If there was no apparat, there was no position. If there was no position, then there was no reason for them to exist, because outside of the apparat, who were they?

Psychologically it is completely understandable that these Party apparatchiks would view the rejection of Communist doctrine and the prospect of the breakdown of the visible, legal structures of Party power (and with them, the collapse of their own careers) as the demise of the USSR, if not the end of the world. When they popularized slogans like "The Fatherland is in danger," it was really the Party apparat and their own positions and privileges that were threatened.

This position was defended, at first glance, somewhat stupidly, and with seeming political insensitivity. But upon examination, the apparatchiks turned out to be quite perspicacious (when it came to their own fates). But alas, it was a perspicacity of the historically doomed. While their hysterical warnings emphasized only the inevitable ruin of the former system of power, they themselves felt they were speaking out about the preservation of power and the need not to "forsake their principles."*

On the other hand, advocates of reform understood that everything had become rotten in the Communist system. They understood as clearly as the conservatives that deprivation of power spelled death for each apparatchik as an individual and for the clan as a whole. These people understood better than anyone else the danger to the secret structures, since they were attached to them in one way or other. But they understood also that the cause of preserving power could be saved only by a radical change of policy, including public rejection of previous state doctrine. They were even prepared to sacrifice the visible part of the Party apparat. But if the reformers could manage to preserve all the secret connections, they could create new legal structures on those foun-

---

*"I Cannot Forsake Principles" was the title of a famous article in the Soviet press by Communist hard-liner Nina Andreyeva that became a cause célèbre for liberals fighting the conservative backlash during the glasnost era. —TRANS.

dations and man them with the more loyal (and flexible) elements within the Party apparat; in that way, they would remain at the head of the state and to some extent preserve "loyalty to the socialist choice"* (and their own ability to allocate material and other riches). This tendency was supported by the flexible (or, to use recent terminology, leftist) "enlightened" politicians among the former Party functionaries and other ideologues.

The collapse, reshuffling, and reconstruction of the ruling apparat which had begun to unfold at the outset of perestroika now picked up speed. Yesterday's Party *nomenklatura* elite—Aleksander Yakovlev, Eduard Shevardnadze, Arkady Volsky, and others—created the Democratic Reform Movement on the ruins of the Party. It was an organization with obvious pretensions to political power. Recently unemployed apparatchiks were invited into the movement, and its platform is strongly reminiscent of the Communist Party's last, social-democratic program, which they had never managed to pass.

Meanwhile, in a number of the former Soviet republics, especially in Central Asia, the Party structures have been preserved untouched, having only changed their names.

In Moscow in 1992, Yury Petrov, a former Central Committee member and secretary of the Sverdlovsk Oblast Party Committee, sits at the head of Boris Yeltsin's administration. Oleg Lobov, another secretary of the same Party committee, is First Deputy Prime Minister of Russia. Viktor Ilyushin, a major Party functionary, is head of the President's secretariat.[26] Mayor Gavriil Popov, himself a former professor of Marxism, appointed as deputy premier of the Moscow government Boris Nikolsky, former second secretary of the Georgian Central Committee. Nikolsky was implicated in the tragic events in Tbilisi in April 1989, when nine people, including women and girls, were massacred by troops

---

*One of the disingenuous arguments which Gorbachev and other (mostly unelected) political figures frequently resorted to was that the population as a whole had already made its "socialist choice" and therefore did not want to make radical market reforms. —TRANS.

using sharpened sappers' shovels and poison gas during the dispersal of a peaceful demonstration.

While there are countless similar examples (especially if we examine the structural changes in the economy), for the time being, we will note only one important fact: all the property of the Communist Party of the Soviet Union—its billions in funds and billions in real estate, all of its sanatoriums, publishing houses, and fleets of cars, and the cooperative enterprises created under its aegis, everything—has been handed over for allocation by the very same new Russian administration that is led by the old secretaries of oblast Party committees.

The simpleminded attempted coup by Party conservatives in August 1991 to halt the unfolding of a process they may well have failed to understand nearly ended tragically. Instead of a gradual transfer of power from the dying Party apparat to a new apparat, a breakdown almost occurred, in which populist forces could have poured in, and then all the secret connections would have been either exposed or destroyed. A start was made in the process of exposure as a broad discussion opened in the press about the Party's gold, about its agents infiltrated (with appropriate subsidies) into the economies of Western countries, and high officials' manipulation of the country's diamonds and gold.

As always happens in such situations, the breakdown had to be repaired with blood and corpses. Interior Minister Boris Pugo, one of the leaders of the coup, committed suicide (or was shot?) before arrest. Two days later, Marshal Sergei Akhromeyev, one of the key figures in the military-industrial complex, hanged himself in his office. We have already noted (Chapter 1) the suicide, in the first days after the putsch, of N. C. Kruchina, general administrator of the Central Committee, who possessed comprehensive information about the secret connections and structures of the Communist apparat. A month and a half later, Georgy Pavlov, general manager of the Central Committee until 1983, jumped from the window of his fashionable apartment building in the center of Moscow. He left no explanations, but he had known at least as much as Kruchina, and according to some reports a great deal more. After this suicide, Telman Gdlyan told the press that Pavlov was one of the key figures of the mafia whose connections had been exposed during the Uzbek Cotton Affair.

These dead took with them all they knew about who really ruled the country and under what conditions.

The two deaths last cited particularly compel us to suspect the existence of some kind of ritual obligation, "suicide as part of the job description." This thought does not seem absurd if we recall the number of suicides of officials that preceded arrests in the Uzbek Cotton Affair.

Testimony on this point was given by Telman Gdlyan, the man in charge of the Uzbek investigation:

"As a professional I understood a certain point in these cases. Mafioso groups have an immutable rule: the best witness is a dead witness.

"For example, we obtained a warrant for the arrest of the [Uzbek] Minister of Internal Affairs, Ergashev, and we drove out to pick him up. But when we got to the site, a command from the Central Committee and the prosecutor's office came down telling us 'Sit on this for a while.' A week goes by. During that time, we tap two phone calls to Ergashev from the Central Committee: 'Gdlyan has come with an arrest warrant—there's no time left. You have to make a courageous decision. We will take care of your family.' On the eve of his arrest, Ergashev calls his family together, says good-bye, and at 7:00 A.M., at the gate of his home, puts a bullet in his temple. That's the kind of method they have, which, by the way, worked wonderfully with Pugo (who knew too much, perhaps), Akhromeyev (I will never believe that a military officer, and what's more, a marshal, would hang himself), and Kruchina, who 'threw himself' out the window (he knew the secret of the 'black Party fund,' including the Party accounts in Swiss banks)."[27]

The thesis about the "businesslike," even "obligatory ritual," nature of the suicide was indirectly confirmed by Ergashev's suicide note: "I am absolutely alone, the son of a poor man, slandered by

Rashidov and his band. I have died an honest member of the CPSU,* a Marxist-Leninist. Long live the CPSU! Marxism-Leninism! Long live the Soviet people! Kudrat."[28]

Mafiosi don't die like that. This is the cry of a hero who covers a land mine with his body. Is it not a war?

In the West, the criminal mafia, which keeps its activities and organization deeply concealed, wages war with governments. But against whom was the ruling Party of our own country, which was essentially the government itself, waging a war? Why would such an ominiscient government need secret structures? From whom was it keeping secrets? After all, isn't the struggle between liberals and conservatives an internal Party struggle? Who is the external enemy, the battle with whom requires blood and death?

*Communist Party of the Soviet Union. —TRANS.

# CHAPTER NINE

*Witness Testimony*

# KGB General Oleg Kalugin

PART ONE

*General Oleg Kalugin was first fired, then stripped of all his titles and awards, for his public exposure of the lawlessness he had witnessed and sometimes participated in during his many years of service in the state security agencies. He began his career as a KGB resident in the United States, and went on to become one of the chiefs of Soviet foreign intelligence. Kalugin was elected to the Supreme Soviet. After the August 1991 failed coup he was restored to his rank as a general.*

LEV TIMOFEYEV: If today all the archives of the KGB were opened, and absolutely everything became known about the KGB, what do you think would shock the public most of all?

OLEG KALUGIN: What would shock the public is the comprehensive, ubiquitous nature of this organization. Many people in our country sense this in their bones, but they would then have this intuitive understanding fully confirmed. And they would be stupefied by the scale, the diversity, the multiplicity, the pervasive nature, of KGB activity. None of this is news exactly, but if the real truth became known, the effect would be staggering. It is one thing to have a general feeling, and it's another when the specific facts are revealed.

LT: Something like that did happen in Poland and Czechoslovakia. The public was so shocked that I believe in Poland a decision was made to seal up these data and close the files for many years, so that it would not instigate a social explosion. Is that true?

OK: That's correct. Because there would be a scandal if the names were named. I know of dozens of very prominent Soviet political and public figures who were agents of the KGB for many years. Even figures in our democratic movement. There are many people in the movement—in fact, famous people—who have been cooperating with the KGB for twenty to twenty-five years. (It's possible, of course, that they have since stopped their cooperation. I do not want to be accused of saying that they are still cooperating today.) Recently I ran into a deputy of the Supreme Soviet, a very prominent person. Suddenly he confessed to me. He apparently thought that I might already know, but just in case, decided to forestall my finding out from other sources. But, as a matter of principle, I am against revealing the list of agents. It would not be in the public interest—with the exception, perhaps, of the rare instance when the activities of such a person today are contrary to the public interest.

LT: But won't the KGB destroy all documents about its past activities?

OK: Not all of them, of course not—but some things are being destroyed. All the dossiers on Solzhenitsyn and Sakharov—many volumes of case files—all of them have been destroyed. What remain are general reports that they were under surveillance by the KGB, with no details of specific circumstances that could make it possible to reliably reconstruct what actually happened.

LT: And documents about political murders? There have been a number of unsolved murders lately which, even if there is no proof of direct KGB participation, at least allow us to speak of the existence of certain social structures, certain clever people who know how to commit murder without leaving clues. There is the murder of Father Aleksandr Men,* for example. For some people, even the death of Sakharov raises doubts.

OK: I think that the KGB hastened Sakharov's departure from this life. I have no doubt about it. I am willing to bet that in Gorky Sakharov was subjected to a certain poison that caused his premature death. I am completely convinced of this, although I have no proof whatsoever. I know that at one time the question of liquidating Solzhenitsyn was discussed. He was in the West by that time. That was stupid, of course. How could anyone reach him in Vermont? He was surrounded by people. Nevertheless, such thoughts never left the minds of our leadership. Furthermore, the initiative here belonged to the Party leaders. The KGB, after all, was the reliable executor of the wishes of the Central Committee. It was precisely the leadership—Suslov, Brezhnev, and Andropov—who could also initiate such actions. And I think that Sakharov's death was helped along by the KGB. I believe that various pharmaceutical preparations were used on him in Gorky. I am sure of this. I am simply extrapolating from those conversations, those intentions, and the point of all of them was to remove him as quickly as possible. How to remove him was a technical matter.

*Popular Russian Orthodox priest known for his liberal views who was found murdered near his home in 1989. The case remains unsolved. —TRANS.

# CHAPTER TEN

*Witness Testimony*

# Elena Bonner,
# Widow of Academician Andrei Sakharov

LEV TIMOFEYEV: You and your husband, of course, always understood that you could simply be murdered. Was that feeling a constant part of your life or did you push it to the side somehow, and decide not to pay it any mind?

ELENA BONNER: The danger always existed, but people cannot live constantly with a feeling of danger. Andrei Dmitrievich and I never tried to hide anything. We never covered the telephone with a pillow to keep anyone from eavesdropping on us.* We were constantly under surveillance, but aside from a few acute situations, it did not affect our lives substantially. This was not some special principle for life, but just the normal way of living. In that sense we lived with more internal calm than most people I know.

LT: The sense that you could be killed, did that threat come from a particular person or persons, or from a certain organization? Did the danger emanate from the KGB?

EB: I don't know whether it was the KGB or the Charity Society.

---

*It is generally believed that the KGB eavesdropped upon conversations in homes through the telephone receiver. —TRANS.

LT: You mean the KGB was not necessarily the embodiment of this danger?

EB: No. I think the KGB has the right structures, but the threat does not always come from them. But I have no proof of this. I am a very emotional person, but at the same time, an incredible rationalist. There are certain fields of knowledge that are not accessible to me, and therefore do not exist for me. I simply live my life. The thought that the danger is from the KGB and not from anyone else is for me a guarantor of psychological security as well. I always need a certain concreteness. Incidentally, that is why many of our friends quarreled with me when I was unwilling to agree with them that Kostya Bogatyrev had been murdered.* I didn't even agree with Andrei about this. Everyone was saying it was so, but I wasn't sure. Perhaps it is a feature of my medical education. There are things that do not exist for me: for example, ESP, the faith healer Yury Kashpirovsky, and other things I know nothing about. No specific religion exists for me.

LT: But at the same time, on the level of your rational perception, can you suppose that the KGB is not the only source of danger?

EB: No, the KGB is not the only source. I don't know who would kill me. Literally every other day, people phone me and say "Just you wait, you old Armenian!" How do I know where the threat is coming from? From Azerbaijanis? And yet, several days ago two men came to see me. They were Azerbaijanis. They brought me roses. And they whispered to me, "Don't think that all of us are like that." I was completely amazed. Those few roses were dearer to me than . . . I don't know . . . baskets full. And they whispered. They were afraid of someone.

---

*Konstantin Bogatyrev (1925–1976), a poet and German translator, was beaten by unknown assailants and died during brain surgery. Some dissidents believe he was attacked by the KGB for his friendship with foreigners. —TRANS.

LT: What does the word "mafia" mean in Russian?

EB: I don't know. You don't have to dig too deeply. A gangsterish process of primitive [capitalist] accumulation is under way. The same structures have the advantage in this, as they have always had the advantage in our lives.

LT: But isn't the process of accumulation dangerous in that anyone at all can grab power?

EB: Everything will be normal. "Anyone at all" will be regulated by all of these financial, fiscal, and other relations. They will become rich, we will remain as poor as we have always been, and a very large part of the country will be destitute. In this process, it is not the scientists and people in the arts—who have lots of money by our standards and have become well-to-do by legal means—who will have the advantage, but the same old apparat. The very same people. Well, they will accumulate capital, and perhaps then they will voluntarily leave power, after becoming Rockefellers and Rothschilds. And then they won't need that formal seat anymore in the Great Kremlin Palace.

LT: Was Sakharov murdered?

EB: I don't know. . . . Will that bring him back? No. Then why get into all of that? Do you understand why I say that? It may seem to some people like indifference to his fate, but it's not. We never knew what was being prepared against us.

LT: Who was preparing it?

EB: How do I know? It was a secret, after all. If you read carefully, we had an incident with my oldest grandson, it's described by Andrei.[29]* But to this day, we don't know what that was. Or the

---

*The family believed that the KGB had poisoned Bonner's grandson on the eve of her departure to Italy for an eye operation. —TRANS.

incident at the eye hospital. My first eye operation was in this country, before I became Andrei's wife. Mikhail Mikhailovich Krasnov, a leading eye surgeon, performed the operation, and did a very good job. I had this ailment from the time I served in the army. I had suffered a contusion, and as a young girl of twenty-two, I was threatened with complete blindness. And for some reason, all the ophthalmologists of the USSR really danced attendance on me. Well, it was really a pity, only twenty-two, the war was over—and then this! And I was a patient of the senior Krasnov, and then his son. Later, after I became Sakharov's wife, I entered the eye hospital once again. One of my classmates worked in the hospital—she was afraid of me, but was still a good woman and had maintained a relationship with me. And I left that Soviet hospital because she called me out of the room and said, "I don't know what they are going to do to you. Get out of here any way you can. The department head asked me to pass this on to you." The next day was Saturday, and I signed myself out. I was forced to get treatment in Italy. Before the trip to Italy, the incident with my grandson Matvei occurred. It was like that all the time. And who did this—how do we know? The mafia, or not, the KGB, or not.

Sometimes I had the feeling that the KGB was provoking us, but we traveled together through many places in the provinces. They could have murdered us. There were times when we were on foot, walking twenty-five kilometers together through the taiga. They could have easily killed us, taken our money, and that would have been it—half of Yakutia are bandits serving terms in exile. But they even seemed to be watching over us sometimes. Who and what, I simply can't say. Therefore, not only do I never try, I never allow myself even to think about trying to find out what I cannot find out. You ask the question of whether Andrei Dmitrievich was murdered or not? I do not know. But proceeding from that, to become obsessed and to devote the rest of my life thinking about this—I can't. All the more because we were both psychologically prepared for such a possibility.

LT: We don't know what happened to Bogatyrev, we don't know what happened to Sakharov, we don't know what happened to Men. . . .

EB: There's a lot we don't know.

LT: But perhaps these murders have some kind of special significance for understanding the entire mechanism of power as a whole?

EB: Perhaps. But it will only become possible to study this seriously when this process of primitive accumulation passes. I am certain that history will be written then, and not today.

LT: Have you ever had direct contact with people about whom you could say unquestionably that they were mafiosi?

EB: I don't think so. Well, perhaps on a petty level. I know a dentist I would call a mafioso. But not seriously. I realize you want some concrete answer. But I'll tell you: Andrei's heart illness was of a type that he could have died very early. It's a disease that usually catches up with people somewhere around the age of forty. In the twenty years I was with him, Andrei Dmitrievich had two periods when his heart condition worsened, and these were not at all in connection with his hunger strikes, as our academicians loved to say.* One time was in 1970, when he could hardly move. The other was in 1975. This illness was not diagnosed in his lifetime, and it was thought that perhaps he'd had a heart attack; that was how it was reported, that he had a myocardial infarction. But the autopsy revealed that in fact he had not had any infarctions. At the moment he died, he had not suffered any worsening of his health. I know that absolutely for a fact. That's all.

*Some academicians at the Soviet Academy of Science would give out misleading reports about Sakharov's condition. —TRANS.

# CHAPTER ELEVEN

# Hatred of Their Own Shadow

In recent times, from the height of various tribunes, from parliamentary podiums to speakers' platforms at rallies, as well as in the press of various persuasions, the name of one common enemy is constantly repeated. This enemy apparently threatens everyone equally—democrats, patriots, apparatchiks, anarchists, monarchists. The slogan "The Fatherland is in danger" has even resounded in some places.

The name of this Public Enemy No. 1, of this social group hated by everyone and antagonistic to everyone, is *teneviki*—dealers in the shadow economy. People say that both the war in the Caucasus and the empty shelves in the stores are on their conscience. Both former apparatchiks and former dissidents are equally intimidated: when the market economy is in full force, then the *teneviki* will seize not only the entire market but power in Russia as well.

It seems as if someone is deliberately whipping up public hatred, but portraying the object of that hatred only in very general terms. Then people are alarmed in a different way. More and more, we hear people saying, "Show us these dealers, show us!" And politicians of various stripes conveniently use the moment to point to *their* enemies and opponents, who in turn dissociate themselves in indignation, and reject the accusations, and then point to *their* accusers. Meanwhile, public expectation is wound up to the limit, and the crowd of impoverished citizens, beginning to be filled with the ranks of unemployed persons, start ranting, "Give them to us!" And they do, they push someone out to the crowd and it doesn't matter if he isn't guilty: "Here's your 'shadow president,' the person to blame for all your tears!"

One has to be careful in naming names and using labels. Using unclear or imprecise political definitions has far more serious consequences than it does in applied linguistics. A mistake can be made with a label one day, and the next day a person could be placed against the wall and shot.

It's not even a question of *teneviki*. Or, at least, they aren't the whole issue. In general, vague definitions are the bane of modern political life. And the most dangerous mistakes occur in the discussion and planning of a strategy for social development. People in Russia are now ashamed of the word "socialism." Russia has almost covered the path from a planned-distributive (administrative-command) system to a free market, but we keep looking back: in the old days, did we really live without the market?

Ask the chairman of a kolkhoz how building materials or spare parts for tractors and cars are procured, and he'll tell you how many bottles of vodka have been drunk, how many buckets of fish soup have been swallowed, how many tubs of honey have been pinched—all this in addition to outright bribes. Ask factory managers how they procure pipes, cement, metal, and glass. Imagine if the middleman, called "the traveling salesman in reverse," were removed from the Soviet economy. This middleman constantly darts around the country, "landing" something, buying someone off, changing one good in short supply for another. Without him—without the raw materials and parts he supplies—the nation's enterprises would have long ago ground to a halt. Is this not the market? Even if it's a black market, it is truly a universal market.

In fact in the last decades in the USSR, not a single product has been manufactured and not a single paid service has been performed outside the confines of the black market. If all of this is the *shadow* economy, where do we look for the real, nonshadow economy? And what do we call it?

It is time to acknowledge forthrightly that in the last decades, there was no "administrative-command" system in our country. It died along with Stalin. In any event, it could not survive long after the emergency conditions of wartime. As soon as the authorities stop shooting people for "sabotage" and giving jail terms for stealing wheat tips, economic logic will always gain the upper hand. No centralized distribution system can take the place of buying and selling. The entire Soviet economy, from top to bottom, is permeated by black-market relationships, which are in fact the living blood circulating in this dead organism. The Communist rulers always controlled these relations, and even cultivated them, understanding very well that they posed no threat whatever to the regime.

The reason the black market posed no threat relates to its chief difference from a free market: profit cannot become full-fledged capital. It cannot "work" to extend production or to increase labor productivity. It could not be used to build a factory or even a workshop and increase production.

If anyone dared to reinvest black-market profits, he was committing what was in the Soviet system the most horrible of crimes: embarking on the dangerous road of free, unrestrained market relations. Rarely did any dealers pursuing such an initiative escape prison; some died. Currently there are some 127,000 persons in Russia serving labor-camp or prison terms for so-called economic crimes. I do not know how many of them were guided by a noble yearning to give people necessary goods, and how many only by a passion for profit, but among them were the best people of the era. We cannot forget Johannes Hint and Nikolai Khudenko,* great reformers who perished as a result of judicial repression. And how many lesser-known dealers in the shadow economy have died? If only these activists, who dared to infringe upon the apparat's

---

*Hint was an Estonian dissident whose case was prosecuted by Telman Gdlyan in the 1970s. Khudenko was another early reformer. Both of them died in labor camp from poor conditions. —TRANS.

monopoly control of even the most minuscule aspects of the economy, had had capital, property, and freedom back then. We can but hope that some of these businessmen have survived.

I can already hear the outraged voices of some readers of high morals. Here I have set about justifying the mafia and advocating that they should be given the opportunity to legally buy land, open factories, and seek profits. I am all for the opportunity for *any* businessman, regardless of his "moral character," to freely (and in any reasonable amounts) buy land, develop the production of goods, and acquire factories or build new ones.

Understandably, it's much more pleasant to associate the word "businessmen" with the Brothers Morozov or the Brothers Tretyakov, the founders of the greatest painting collections in Russia. But who among my respected readers and visitors to the Tretyakov galleries or the Museum of Fine Art knows the source of the original capital used to acquire these collections, which have now become our national treasures? I ask this not because I know something bad about the nature of those family fortunes, but in order to make the point that capital is indifferent to morals. As soon as money is taken from the cash box and goes to work for production, it loses whatever criminal stink it may have. Yes, you say, but what about historical retribution? They stole the money, and now they are millionaires.

We must sadly admit that there will be no historical retribution. If someone has committed a crime and been caught in the act, then of course he should go to court. But historical retribution has no relationship to law. The experience of socialism in Russia has proved that either we think about retribution, about expropriation of the expropriators, or we work toward a productive market economy and private property. Either/or—not both. In the market, the moral history of each individual's capital is strictly a family matter. We will leave to writers the moral character of future Russian Cowperwoods and Forsytes. Society, however, needs a productive economy.

The conception of Soviet reality as one of the "administrative-command" system comes from belles lettres. But fortunately novelists have been mistaken. The anti-utopias of Zamyatin, Huxley, and Orwell could no more come true than utopias themselves. No force or brainwashing could possibly take away a person's need for the simple relations of buying and selling; there is simply no other mechanism in nature for the maintenance of life for *Homo sapiens.*

The Communists suffered defeat primarily because they could not destroy the market. Everything—including Party positions—could be bought and sold in our country. You could even purchase the right to have a newly discovered planet named after you.

With the inexorable consistency of economic logic, the ruling apparat itself became a market commodity. Everything had its own price list. If I asked how much the seat of a district committee secretary somewhere in Central Asia or the Caucasus cost, the answer would depend on the kind of district—city or rural, etc. If Party seats were a commodity on the black market, then what can be said about the position of kolkhoz chairman or factory director. A story recently ran in the press how in one oblast fourteen police jobs were purchased for money.

These are not exceptions—this is the very system under which we have lived. (It has been partially preserved even to this day.) Appointments were not always paid for openly, with money changing hands; in some cases, someone who was loyal, who the system felt was "our kind of guy," ended up in a lucrative position and how he paid for it depended on his quick-wittedness. In thirty years of reporting trips through agricultural regions, I never once met an official whose family bought food in a regular store.

The entire Soviet system—everything without exception—was nothing more than an enormous black market in goods, services, positions, and privileges. No, perhaps it's the reverse—positions, privileges, and then, in last place, goods. The material result is hardly the main point of the system. The main goal is to hang on to power. Whenever some enthusiast, like Nikolai Khudenko, has promised to raise the productivity of labor by a factor of three or five, but outside the existing system, this was seen as a direct threat to the powers-that-be, and that enthusiast was killed. And in this reverse priority, in this twisted logic, lies the whole essence of the Soviet political and economic system, the whole essence of socialism.

We will not forget this wonderful, historically capacious word. Neither Marx nor Lenin, nor their contemporaries, ever heard of the "administrative-command" system, but they spoke about socialism a great deal. They understood socialism as first and foremost a negation of the sacred right to private property.

It was precisely socialism that we had in the Soviet Union and still have to a significant degree in Russia and the other former republics. There was no private property, and essentially, there still isn't. The means of production belong to no one: they are "the state's" (or no one's). Nothing seriously belongs to anyone—except power. It is not property that is allocated among the citizens of the country, but power—power over land, factories, forests, and railroads, power over valuables that belong to no one. This includes power over the work force and power over other human beings, the sweetest form of power there is. All this is the prerogative of office. To it are added such minor considerations as material privileges. Thus it is that a position (objectified power) is the basic market commodity. The consistent realization of the idea of socialism is in fact the shadow economy, and not the "fourth dream of Vera Pavlovna"* or the "administrative-command" system.

The ideal conditions for divergent mafia structures arise in the shadow of the commodityless market of power. Hence our well-known fears for the future: with the transition to new conditions of ownership, the advantage will once again accrue to those who are in official seats. It is easier for them to get the necessary permits, to acquire property, and to fend off their rivals.

While their advantages will continue to exist, is there some vestige here of the class view of the order of things? Having already defined the Party apparat as a class of expropriators, some

*The dream of a character in Nikolay Chernyshevsky's *What Is to Be Done?* of a happy socialist future. Dostoyevsky polemicizes with this positive vision of socialism in "Raskolnikov's Dream" in *Crime and Punishment.* —TRANS.

politicians are not content with merely overthrowing them or confiscating their unearned property. They would like to relegate the apparatchiks to the disfranchised class as in the 1930s—if not shoot them.

So, is history repeating itself? And will there be talk once again of historical retribution?

I have no sympathy for the Party apparat, but I do admit that I would like to see justified the worst fears of those who worry that yesterday's apparatchiks will turn into tomorrow's property owners—yes, justified! That would be wonderful! Let them buy land. Let them create cooperatives or joint stock companies. Let them become owners and compete. Let them receive dividends and reinvest them in production. Let them become rich entrepreneurs. Even let them fail. Because to become an entrepreneur means to reject power by position and throw oneself into the risky seas of market competition. In the marketplace the strongest person is not he who takes away from others, but he who sells more. Let them trade. Let them become useful at last. I do not understand why they do not have a right to this—as long as they don't prevent anyone else from doing the same thing.

The problem is that they aren't in fact becoming private owners of land or enterprises. They simply do not know how to make themselves into honest entrepreneurs. Fearing those who do know how, they seek to maintain their monopoly on power, and stand in the way of change in the country with the help of the conspiratorial structures and the new mafia.

Business people who do not want to link their future with the secret organizations of the former Party apparat sense this better than others. They understand perfectly well that the problem is not, as some Russian and Western economists believe, that market structures are underdeveloped. To the contrary, declares Konstantin Borovoy, chief manager of the Russian Raw Materials and Commodities Exchange, "market structures in our country are sufficiently developed. They have long been capable of assuming all the functions of the collapsed state structures. The problem is that there are no property owners. Now as always, bureaucrats—from the

President down to the chairmen of local government executive committees—do not want to give anything up. They understand that if a real property owner comes on the scene, they will have to prove their usefulness, and that they can't tolerate at all."[30]

Borovoy notes that young businessmen are being accused of making money through brokerage rather than investment in production. To which he responds that "we would be happy to become producers. But they won't let us! Our commodities exchange is the largest commercial organization. Yet all its property is rented. Even if we wish, we cannot buy land and start production—modern-day feudal lords block our path. And when the people's patience finally runs out, the feudal lords will try to sic them on us. But a popular rebellion will sweep them away first."[31]

Today, whenever politicians or economists or practical businessmen gather to talk, the question inevitably comes back to property. In whose hands are held the material riches of Russia, and who in reality controls the economy, and along with it the political destiny of the country?

How sad it is to read about the missed opportunities of Russia. "On the next day everything was taken care of in the best way possible. Skudronzhoglo cheerfully gave 10,000 without interest, without collateral, simply for a signature. Thus was he so ready to help put anyone on the path to ownership. He showed Chichikov all of his estate."* Cheerfully gave 10,000—and without finding out anything about the character of the borrower, although here was certainly a dealer in the shadow economy!

Will we ever see our people "on the path to ownership"? What kind of unfortunate nation are we that the negative model of our history was the ridiculous Chichikov, and the positive model was neither Skudronzhoglo nor Levin,† but the even more ridiculous Rakhmetov and Bazarov?‡

---

*From Gogol's *Dead Souls.* —TRANS.
†From Tolstoy's *Anna Karenina.* —TRANS.
‡The nihilists from Chernyshevsky's *What Is to Be Done?* and Turgenev's *Fathers and Sons.* —TRANS.

Recently an influential American magazine published a list of the 100 greatest Americans of the twentieth century. Almost a third of them were businessmen and entrepreneurs. They included the head of an automobile corporation, the founder of a computer industrial empire, and the president of an aircraft design firm of world renown. For us Russians it would be easier to select 100 great evildoers. Furthermore, they would all be lovers of the truth and great specialists in historical retribution.

How can we fully realize that we are a society with a sick mind? It is the intelligentsia, the public conscience, that is the source of the illness. The chief symptom is the mania for *uravnilovka*, egalitarianism, or bringing everyone down to one level. ". . . the interests of distribution and equality in the consciousness and feelings of the Russian intelligentsia always dominated over the interests of production and creativity," wrote the philosopher Nikolai Berdyayev more than eighty years ago. He could easily have been writing about exactly those politicians today who are obsessed with social justice and who are always looking around to see if the burden on the shoulders of the worker is too great.

It is unbearably great. The mania for *uravnilovka* and the imposition of the ideas of prohibition inevitably spawn the black market, and the criminal psychology of the ruling apparat along with it. The more each entrepreneur with initiative is held back, the greater that burden will be. It is not a question of the peculiarities of the Russian national psychology, but the very destiny of the nation itself. Will we remain a great people or will we be extinguished in the historical record, remaining in the memory of future generations only as a ridiculous psychological phenomenon of the twentieth century?

# CHAPTER TWELVE

*Witness Testimony*

# KGB General Oleg Kalugin

PART TWO

LEV TIMOFEYEV: You have repeatedly spoken about the complete dependency of the KGB on the Party apparat.

OLEG KALUGIN: It's interdependent. They are grafted together. There's a symbiosis. It is a Party-police system.

LT: But it seems that the Party apparat has collapsed before our very eyes. What happened to the KGB?

OK: The KGB is the most stable part of the integrated structure. The state security agencies were always the preservers of the foundations. In this case, the system can disintegrate and the foundations can be subjected to the most complete change, but the structure created to work under any conditions continues to work automatically. Although the processes of peeling away and disintegration are also at work there, for the KGB authorities it is a question of preserving not only the system itself, but themselves. It's a question of self-defense and survival. The KGB will be one of those structures that will struggle until the end. And that's the danger.

LT: Many people say that with the destruction of the surface structure, the Party apparat is trying to preserve some invisible part or even to create something new—for example, to go into the economic sphere, and to seize property and create associations, companies, and firms that would belong to the former structures, but which would preserve or even acquire new political meaning and new political strength. Does the KGB take part in this?

OK: Yes, they take part actively. My colleagues virtually control the privatization process, the process of creating joint ventures, and the process of creating joint stock or other types of non-state companies. I could name specific organizations for you—for example, the state cooperative association ANT. Remember the scandalously infamous ANT? Twenty KGB officers were assigned to it—officially. They held positions in this association. These were not young lieutenants, but mature people of fairly high rank. Imagine what kind of corporation it was, sanctioned by Prime Minister Ryzhkov, with the participation of the KGB. It was a powerful economic conglomerate, which took everything into itself—the Party, state structures, and the military-industrial complex.

LT: And what about Ivan Polozkov, who so loved to expose ANT? Did that mean he was in conflict with the KGB?

OK: ANT was created here, in Moscow. It was sanctioned by the highest Soviet agencies. But Polozkov was making use of information from a local KGB administration in Krasnodar. This served as the basis for enormous political speculation. Polozkov made a name for himself as a supposed standard-bearer of the people's interests, but at the same time he tried to break up new structures emerging on our economic horizon. The local KGB agents went into action (which usually happens in the provinces), under the direction of the Territory Party Committee Secretary—that is, Polozkov. And the affair snowballed. When a public scandal occurs, it is hard to cover up the tracks. They found a scapegoat in the person of Vladimir Ryashentsev* and some fairly petty figures.

*See pages 124–29. —TRANS.

Ryzhkov had to make some explanations, but on the whole, the people who were behind the affair remained in the shadows; no one knows them.

Incidentally, Polozkov reflects certain ultra-right sentiments in the Communist Party. The Krasnodar KGB is absolutely in solidarity with him; the head there was a certain Vailenko, who is now secretary of a branch of the Union of Writers in Kuban.

LT: Is that a promotion or a demotion?

OK: He retired and received that position as a sinecure.

LT: So if I have understood correctly, the ANT case revealed a conflict between those who wanted to possess and run everything in the old way and those who look for new routes in order not to lose everything.

OK: That's correct. It's essentially the attempt of two flanks of the same old Party to find a way out of the situation. Some are seeking the truth in the preservation of old positions, and others are looking for new forms of power, including the power of ownership. Today, they are basically involved in trying to turn the property, buildings, and real estate belonging to Party agencies into profits. This is not so much for the Party's sake as it is for self-preservation. The most typical mercantile inclinations. I would like to emphasize that this is not so much a desire to create new Party structures outside the framework of the traditional ones as it is a desire to preserve the Party's power, a panicked flight to the private sector in order to maintain their standard of living.

LT: I think your point of view on these events is optimistic. Are you really talking about the assimilation of the Party apparat to a normal market system?

OK: The market will be occupied by the ruling apparat and the KGB, because they have the opportunities to control the processes of privatization and the creation of new enterprises. They have the licenses, they have the influence. But this exodus into economic structures is an escape of rats from a ship.

LT: Let's suppose that this flight has taken place. They have grabbed everything they can possibly get their hands on, and as you have put it, have fled from the ship. But is this really like fleeing from a ship? Is it true that these people will then become independent from Party structures that helped them acquire property or open a business? If this is just a collapse, corruption, and disintegration, and the former Party apparat becomes a group of irresponsible private owners, that's one thing. I don't know whether it is good or bad. But couldn't it happen that the Party apparat would in a sense delegate its people into the economy, provide them with property, and promote them in the market, but also maintain control over them, over the market, and finally over the country? That's another thing altogether.

OK: I understand. I agree that there is an element of panicky self-preservation here, a struggle to keep the organizational nucleus in this panic and confusion, to preserve people who may in a certain situation once again emerge on the political scene and try to bring back what they have lost. That is, I would not say that this is a mere "escape from the ship"—that would be too simplistic. There is undoubtedly an element here of an organized retreat. But still I think that in the overwhelming majority of cases this is a retreat of people looking for opportunities to preserve their previous standard of living.

LT: If you use the word "organized" here, then you should be talking not about a retreat, but an invasion. An invasion of Communists in the market economy of the future?

OK: No, it's still a retreat, under which the retreating force tries to maintain some element of order and the possibility of preserving a nucleus, and then perhaps, in time, returning to the past.

LT: What is the KGB's place in this process?

OK: They are like the captain who is the last one to flee the ship.

LT: Perhaps current or former KGB officers will be the ones to make up the nucleus of the future relapse?

OK: Perhaps. Why did the KGB and the Party work in such close tandem? The Party people never came out of the underground. They were always conspirators and they created parallel structures, both legal and illegal. And now that experience will come in handy. As far as conspiracy goes, the KGB is the best assistant. They have people who are professionals at conspiracy. In that sense, the KGB's experience will be invaluable for those who are attempting, without panic, to preserve the conspiratorial political structures.

LT: In the KGB structures, were there or are there any organizations or research centers that are studying these possibilities?

OK: I don't know if there are any today. But if I were still there, I would think about it seriously.*

LT: Are there any secret social forces, structures, or movements in the country that could attempt to take political power? For example, people mention the *teneviki*, the dealers on the black market.

OK: I think that the *teneviki* are the latest scarecrow our system has created. Many black-market dealers are getting rich, but do they really want to get involved in politics? What do they need that for? I am acquainted with people from these spheres. They are all fairly

*This interview took place in July 1991. In September 1991, Kalugin returned in an advisory role to the KGB.

primitive people who have accumulated their riches partly through cleverness and partly through audacity. But to consider them some kind of political force in the country—I assure you, that is not true. If you make our economy a normal market economy, the shadow structure will simply evaporate into it.

# CHAPTER THIRTEEN

# Wild Privatization

Under the changing circumstances, Party conservatives struggled simplemindedly to hang on, if not to their principles, then at least to the privileges slipping out of their hands. The well-publicized scandal around the privatization of dachas outside Moscow was a clear, textbook example of this phenomenon.

The case was quite simple. Just outside Moscow, there are enormous expanses of picturesque lands on riverbanks, or on the edge of forests. These are tracts set aside for dachas; sometimes whole villages of dachas allocated to various levels of Party, economic, army, and other state agencies. There are thousands of hectares of superlative properties which belonged before the revolution to the tsar's family or his relatives. In modern times, billions of rubles have been invested in constructing and outfitting the homes, and millions are spent annually subsidizing the development and maintenance of the dacha establishments.

The dacha is the symbol of a Soviet bureaucrat's success. According to an unwritten but immutable law, a person acquires a dacha immediately after taking an official position. The quality of the country home also changes according to the position. If an official succeeds in his career and is advanced in his job, he moves to a better dacha. The higher the office, the more luxurious the home, the larger the yard behind the fence, and the more numerous the servants. But there is also a reverse relationship. If you are fired from your job or leave the position, farewell, dacha! It's been that way under Stalin, under Khrushchev, and under Brezhnev. The government dacha was not only a symbol of privilege, but a sign of completely personal dependency of the Party official on the entire system as a whole.

When the foundations were shaken, *nomenklatura* officials (like all Soviet citizens) sensed the winds of freedom. Who could fail to understand their desire, on the one hand, to free themselves from dependency, and on the other hand, to liberate themselves in such a way as to retain their privileges? It seemed possible to resolve this dilemma by purchasing the valuable dacha homes as private property for an insignificant, purely symbolic sum along with the enormous land tracts that went with them.

There were many press stories about this sort of arrangement, but nowhere was the true scale of the operations revealed, since no one estimated the real cost of the properties. This is also a certain psychological phenomenon. A person knows how much money and effort need to be spent on building a home; he knows how much a home, a barn, or a garage costs if purchased at market prices—there is a market in this type of real estate. But no conception exists of the cost of a land tract, since never under Soviet power had there existed a land market. Tracts of land for construction were always allocated for free by administrative decision. (Even so, an ordinary person had to pay enormous bribes to officials at various levels, but we are speaking here of the highest-ranking officials, who did not pay such bribes.)

Even the current muckrakers in the democratic press talk about the affair as involving dachas, mentioning the land only in passing. Just one instance from the Uzbek Cotton Affair, perhaps not even the most significant, is fairly illustrative of the value put on dachas. It involves Gossnab, the State Supply Office—one of the most corrupt organizations in the Party economic system. It was to Gossnab that Vakhab Usmanov brought some gold bangles, to obtain the allocations of resources and materials needed for his cotton ministry:

"In 1990, sixty-six state dachas were sold to high-level employees of USSR Gossnab with the participation of Minister Anisimov; the minister bought a dacha for himself for 8,600 rubles, although its cost was much higher. . . . In 1991 seventy-six dachas with furniture were sold to high-level Gossnab employees. The cost of each home was no higher than 5,000 rubles, although even by the most modest estimates, the value is many times higher. Along with the dachas, the owners received cost free more than fifty tracts of land."[32]

How much was stolen?

For more than 142 dachas outside Moscow, and the 71 hectares of land with them, about 1.5 million rubles were paid (by the 1990 exchange rate, about $75,000). It would be difficult to say how much the market value would be today for these luxurious Moscow suburban properties, but most likely each one of the 142 tracts could be sold at an auction for no less than $30,000. So we could speak about more than $4 million being stolen.

The dacha scandal was about to catch fire, but then sputtered. It turned out that everything had been done strictly according to law—according to Soviet law, where having permission to acquire an item is important, and its market value is not. The hand of the state does whatever it wishes.

The dacha scandal was only an insignificant episode in a system-wide struggle for survival, which people of the Party, economic, and administrative apparatus waged and continue to wage under the new conditions. They understood long ago that no political measures could help them to preserve power in its previous forms and structures. While they still have some levers of power in their hands, they are using them primarily for building their own future. So as not to lose continuity, so that the bubble doesn't burst, they link the past with the future, connecting their futures with the market entrepreneurial life of tomorrow. Even while they have been denouncing private property and striving by any means (including crude pressure on the President) to delay the complete legalization of privatization, they understand the inevitability of such a step and are trying to grab as much private property for themselves as they possibly can.

The old apparat's involvement with capitalist structures—its creeping takeover of and outright merging with them—is called "wild privatization" by ordinary people. Basically, for a brief time, people of the Party and other *nomenklatura* both acquired the freedom of private initiative and preserved their entire distributive power over state property.

For example, several years ago, the press mentioned that the Finance Minister of the Ryzhkov government, fifty-three-year-old Valentin Pavlov (who later became Prime Minister and a leader of the 1991 coup), had taken the post of chairman of the board of a newspaper publishing consortium called Business World (whose original investment fund was more than 10 million rubles). Mikhail Bocharov, chairman of the High Economic Council of the RSFSR, was also president of a concern called Butek.[33]

While the politics of Pavlov and Bocharov are diametrically opposed—the latter is one of the leaders of the reformists and democrats—they have turned out to have the same interests.

We do know something about Pavlov and Bocharov, but nothing about Business World, Butek, or the other firms with which our current politicians are connected. We have absolutely no knowledge of how deeply the politicians are involved in them, or how dependent they are on hidden ties. How do these connections, this dependence, influence political decisions? (For surely they must.)

True, Moscow figures and their connections are one way or another in the public eye, but in the provinces, wild privatization becomes an overtly criminal activity. A typical report from Novosibirsk Oblast:

Local executive committees were virtually never under the control of elected bodies, the soviets. They were subordinate to Party committees. This provided fertile ground for corruption, since all power in the region is in the district soviets and executive committees. With the aid of these local government structures, instead of privatization, state property is being grabbed right and left.

V. P. Gorbunov was first deputy of the district executive committee in its previous incarnations. When it became clear to him that he could not continue to work with the newly constituted

soviet,* he voluntarily resigned and became the general director of
an inter-industry joint stock company called Energia. Before his
departure, he "organized" a decision by the executive committee
to transfer several buildings that belonged to the district (buildings
covering a total area of 3,500 square yards), to Energia. That is, he
simply gave himself a present.

Energia was created with the avowed positive aim of constructing housing for the public at large. But at one of the sites that had
been illegally impounded, a commercial secondhand store was
opened; the other buildings remained empty. In other words, the
former first deputy chairman of a district executive committee,
who may well have retained his Party membership, was busy
making money. Each day, stores like this one and others bring him
new profits, which can be used to purchase more state property
that is being privatized.

Each time a district soviet tried to offer a building on very
profitable terms, it would often turn out that the building had been
deeded to someone and was already occupied. Such deeds were
given only to connected insiders. In many cases, the shadow of the
old guard loomed behind these illegal transactions.

It is also incredibly difficult to stop the mafia from gaining illegal
profits. They do not blink at blackmail, or intimidation, or murder,
or even attempts to discredit the legally elected authorities. For
example, a Swedish pharmaceutical firm offered to rent a building
for foreign currency. Besides the rent, the firm promised to fund a
soup kitchen for the poor for $10,000 per month, and to install
medical equipment at a district hospital free of charge. The advantages for the district seemed obvious. But suddenly a rumor started
up about some alleged violation of foreign currency regulations,
although none such had in fact occurred. When the slander did not
stick, recourse was had to other methods: four thugs with brass

*In multicandidate elections in 1989–1990, many non-Communists and
democrats were elected to the district soviets—representative bodies similar
to town councils. The district executive committees—the administrative
staffs of district offices—were technically unaffected by the elections, but in
many cases were forced to leave when democrats came to power. —TRANS.

knuckles lay in wait for the person upon whom the decision depended and assaulted him at the entrance of his home.

Pilfering has escalated to massive proportions. According to some reports, anywhere from 20 to 50 percent of produce is regularly stolen from district warehouses. Farmer's markets are under the control of criminal elements, who extract a commission from each seller and force sellers to keep their prices above a certain level. District KGB and police departments report that the bandits are well armed.[34]

In the old days, people in the ruling apparat could pursue their private economic gain only through black-market dealings, through direct or indirect ties with shadow capital. But new, more or less legal, and quite productive opportunities have now appeared for the merging of interests, cooperatives and joint stock companies with mixed capital. People in the *nomenklatura* are present in two capacities—as representatives of official power structures and as private entrepreneurs.

The term "wild privatization" has gained currency in Russia to describe the spontaneous effort of yesterday's apparatchiks to seize as much for themselves as possible and turn it into private property. A popular current pun plays on the Russian words *privatizatsia* (privatization) and *prikhvatizatsia* (from the verb *prikhvatit*, to grab). But *prikhvatizatsia* is not primarily a matter of financial maneuvers by individual Party bureaucrats. The fact is that long before the collapse of aboveground Party structures in August 1991, apparatchiks were carefully planning political action to preserve the maximum of power in secret Party structures.

One major embodiment of this planning is to be found in a Central Committee resolution of August 23, 1990, "On Emergency Measures to Organize Commercial and Foreign Economic Activity of the Party":

It appears that the following measures should be taken immediately in order to secure conditions for the launching of commercial and foreign economic activity by the Party at the level of its central agencies:

—assignment of a Politburo member or Central Committee secretary to act as the Party treasurer, empowered to handle matters concerning the production, financial, and commercial activity of the Party, including foreign economic activity;

—preparation of proposals to create some new "interim" economic structures (foundations, associations, etc.), with minimal "visible" ties to the Central Committee, which could become focal points of the "invisible" Party economy;

—immediate preparation of plans for using anonymous organizations to mask direct links to the Party when launching commercial and foreign economic Party activity; in particular, consideration of the possibility of merging with already functioning joint ventures, international consortiums, etc., through capital investment;

—consideration of ways and means of establishing a bank controlled by the Central Committee with the right to conduct hard-currency operations, the investment of the Party's hard-currency reserves in international firms controlled by friends of the Party;[*]

—consultations with the USSR State Supply Office on the use of Soviet property remaining after the withdrawal of forces from Czechoslovakia, Hungary, and East Germany, for foreign economic cooperation;

—creation of a consulting firm with the status of a legal entity, but without direct links to the Central Committee apparat, for the practical organization of economic cooperation and the provision of brokerage services for foreign economic activity of various Party organizations and the commercial firms of fraternal parties.[35]

Although the old Party apparatus has deeply concealed its underground structures, it cannot hide completely from public scrutiny. A number of ardent and determined people have managed

[*]I.e., Communist parties abroad. —TRANS.

to get past all the contrived roadblocks to ferret out the Party mafia's conspiratorial plans. Among these investigators are Sergei Aristov and his senior colleague Vladimir Dmitriev, both with the Russian Prosecutor's Office.

As Aristov has said: "In the summer of 1991, a giant, finely tuned 'invisible' Party economy, corruptly involved to the necessary degree with the current government, went underground. At the beginning of 1991, the visible, legal part of this iceberg alone consisted of almost eight million rubles. How much did they manage to hide?"[36]

The investigators possess a curious file with a telling order written on it: "One hundred million taken. Hide it." Beneath the order is the signature of a very prominent person, which the prosecution is for the time being withholding in the interests of the ongoing investigation. The contents of the file are even more intriguing. There is a list of candidates who are eligible, in the opinion of the Central Committee, for the role of Party representatives who are to hold power of attorney. Aristov and Dmitriev surmise that during the confusion of the August coup, this file managed to "slim down" by about 80 percent.

Taking all this into account, on October 10, 1991, the prosecutor's office opened criminal case No. 18/6220-91. Investigators believe that the Party's trusted agents have three main sources of income: anonymous enterprises in the Commonwealth of Independent States; anonymous Western firms in developed countries; and various dealings in securities deposited in major world banks.

*Source number one:* Aristov's investigation group has found more than a hundred commercial Party enterprises in Moscow, and about six hundred, all told, throughout Russia. Among the directors of these shadowy Party firms are people who have substantial influence in the current legitimate government.

Using the example of one small enterprise, Aristov and Dmitriev tracked a typical scheme for laundering money stolen by apparatchiks. An enterprise would be registered under a dummy corporation, after which it would obtain several hundred million rubles in credit at the Central Committee's Administrative Department. After this transaction, the funds began a life of their own. But the note of credit, and thus the invisible lines of control over the enterprise's future, remains in the hands of former Party bureaucrats.

Great hopes were placed in commercial banks. The investigation discovered twelve banks controlled by the Party, with deposits of more than 1.5 billion rubles. Tens of millions were found in the reserves of the USSR Bank of Trade Unions and the Tokobank. The largest Party bank is the Autobank, which has received a deposit of one billion rubles from the Party, on which it pays interest.

*Source number two:* According to Aristov and Dmitriev, the prosecution possesses documents about many firms in the West which have been incorporated with Party funds. These firms have a simple modus operandi: a company will be sold, say, a certain amount of oil or armaments for a modest price. Then it resells these goods at world market prices. The difference goes into a bank account.

*Source number three:* There are many bank accounts abroad. So far, this is the only conclusion the investigators can make with certainty.

Some documents in Case No. 18/6220-91 are so expressive that they require no commentary. For example:

Personal Obligation to the Communist Party
I (last name, first name), a member of the Communist Party since (date of entry), with Party card (number), do certify with this document that I have, after due consideration, voluntarily decided to become a representative agent of the Party and to fulfill the duties entrusted to me by the Party in any post and in any circumstance without revealing my membership in the body of such agents. I pledge to keep and use carefully in the interests of the Party the financial and material means entrusted to me, and guarantee to return them immediately upon demand.

I acknowledge as Party property everything earned by me as a result of economic activity using Party funds, and guarantee that I will remit such earnings, at any time to any place, as ordered. I pledge to observe strict confidentiality regarding information entrusted to me and to fulfill the assignments of the Party given to me through authorized persons.

July 1991.[37]

What debts (and thus political obligations) may be called in one fine day by the secret structures that hold such signed statements?

This "privatization with a blessing" turns out to be so profitable so invariably that competition springs up with a political agenda—one of influencing directly the decisions of executive and legislative authority in the country. For example, let's look closely now at the case of the state cooperative firm ANT, which was commanded by twenty KGB officers, according to General Kalugin.

Perhaps the most important feature of ANT and its directors was complete loyalty to the Communist government. The organizer and head of ANT was Vladimir Ryashentsev, a former KGB officer with extensive ties to both the state security agencies and the defense industry (he had worked for a time as the head of security at a "closed"—that is, secret—factory, most likely a defense plant). Ryashentsev had mastered the essential principles of the economic system: the people who reap the profits aren't those who fight for the abolition of bans and restrictions but those who know how to get around the restrictions and who share their bounty with the authorities who make the restrictions. If you don't just barge ahead but operate with intelligence and discretion, you can cut in some very high officials—even the prime minister himself. By buying yourself the privilege of violating the restrictions, you can earn more (and with less risk) than you could even under free-market competition. The risk was especially low in the case of ANT, since the government needed the cooperative a lot more than the cooperative needed the government.

ANT was born in 1987, at the very beginning of perestroika, as soon as even a feeble opportunity appeared for independent business initiatives. They began with the "small change" traditional for cooperatives—a sewing-machine factory making parts for Zhiguli cars—and ended with billion-ruble deals involving the sale of military technology abroad and delivery of luxury items to Russia. Furthermore, as those involved in the affair themselves say, from the very beginning, they were also involved in scientific designs commissioned by defense enterprises—most likely, helped by Ryashentsev's old ties.

Meanwhile, we should not lose sight of what Kalugin has told us, that ANT was originally created with the assistance of the KGB. This is not to denigrate the personal business abilities of Ryashentsev; he apparently continues to enjoy a solid reputation as one of the most capable, influential, and successful businessmen in Russia.

Almost from the first, ANT was supported by Politburo member Yegor Ligachev, who at the time was number two in the Party. Having acquainted himself with the cooperative's activities, Ligachev made an oracular pronouncement: "I think that these fellows are building the kind of socialist cooperation that Lenin contemplated."[38] We may suppose that what actually impressed Ligachev was the cooperative's readiness to cut the Communist government itself into the deal—and provide a front for involvement in commerce by Ryzhkov's and Ligachev's people. Ryashentsev was interested not so much in the percentage returned as profits as in the overall volume of turnover. At one point he stated that he would be entirely satisfied with 1 to 3 percent of ANT's profits, with the rest going to the government. And that, apparently, was their agreement.

We have to understand the Communist government as well here. In keeping with principles "which could not be forsaken," they declared in 1989 a ban on middlemen and trade and purchase cooperatives, deeming such activity speculation. The accompanying prosecution of middlemen virtually closed them down throughout the country. But there were, after all, some economists in the government who weren't dull bureaucrats; they realized that without the activity of middlemen, the economy wouldn't work—in fact, middlemen's activities probably represented the most profitable area of the economy. Therefore, for the sake of their own profits, it became possible to forsake their own principles.

ANT soon took on the job of serving as a middleman in deals involving foreign partners. The business turned out to be incredibly profitable for the government, Ryashentsev, and those who earned profits from the cooperative. They were not in private business but actually supported those Communist programs which restricted, restrained, and tried to stamp out real private business.

"The French financial group CDC discovered us through a computer club," said Ryashentsev. "This group proposed delivering a large shipment of computer technology for Soviet rubles. We asked the French: 'Do you sell only computers?' The answer came back: 'We can sell clothing, medical equipment, anything you want, anything you need.' This was on the eve of 1989.

"The deal was so profitable," Ryashentsev told a reporter, "that we reported to the Council of Ministers."

I was summoned to one of the agencies. After the first few words, I understood that the government approved of our proposed operation with CDC.

Furthermore, CDC agreed to keep the accounts at the official exchange rate of 62 kopecks to the dollar. If we take into account the real cost of the dollar, then the profit would prove to be enormous, of course.

But it was a profitable business for the French as well: they were interested in metals, trucks, chemicals, timber, and recyclable materials.

Representatives from the Council of Ministers flew with me to Paris. In order not to give the visit an overly official cast, they were registered as employees of the ANT cooperative.

We returned from Paris in March 1989. Prime Minister Nikolai Ryzhkov signed an official order to create the ANT concern. We were allowed to perform barter operations— that is, to exchange one commodity for another, with the accounts in rubles.

In September, on the basis of that document, we were
allowed to purchase so-called unliquidated materials, products that had been manufactured above the plan, including
from defense ministry enterprises.

On October 6, a new government order was issued to
permit ANT unlicensed export.

Our partners abroad made deliveries to us charged
against our future export. Within only a half year, imported
goods worth 30 billion rubles were to appear on the market. But someone did not want the shortages to begin to
end. Who?[39]

Ryashentsev posed this rhetorical question after ANT had already virtually ceased to exist, without ever having got the
chance to unleash its enormous potential as a middleman. Unquestionably, rivals cut them down—but who? And from where,
from the economic or the political realm? What level of competition could there be, especially when we keep in mind that the
state cooperative firm ANT was itself a "post office box"—that
is, a closed, secret enterprise with a "first department"* and other
KGB services, as was required? What is more, one of the first
local Party organizations within the economy's cooperative sector was created in ANT; in Moscow alone, 110 Communist
Party members were registered. Who could have competed with
such an enterprise? Surely not the democratic opposition, which
was nowhere near as powerful as Prime Minister Ryzhkov, Politburo member Ligachev, and the KGB itself. Then who? What
forces possess such might in the country? In order to venture a
guess, we must look closely at how ANT, speaking in the here
completely appropriate language of the underworld, was "tech-
nologically outfitted."

At some point, the ANT bosses made an agreement with a

*The personnel department in most Soviet factories and institutions,
which is always controlled by the KGB. —TRANS.

certain Major General Dovgan, general director of the Vzlyot association, about delivery abroad of some tractors supposedly refashioned out of tanks manufactured by ANT. But when ANT's shipment, dispatched from a Ural factory, arrived at the port of Novorossisk, it turned out to consist of tanks, still fully armed.

This was when scandal broke out. Through *Sovetskaya Rossiya*, the organ of Party conservatives, the entire country learned that some cooperative businessmen had become so outrageous that they were selling military technology—the very might of the country—abroad. Ivan Polozkov, then First Secretary of the Krasnodar Territory Party Committee, made fierce accusations from the podium of the USSR Congress of People's Deputies. Simultaneously, the internal Party police—the Party Control Commission, headed by Boris Pugo—took up the case. It was also transferred to the prosecutor's office and an investigation was opened (which dragged on for months without results).

Meanwhile, by December 1990 a parallel investigation had been taken up by newspapers and magazines, and this was successful: it was established indisputably that the tanks were sent deliberately. The affair was a bald-faced, cleverly executed provocation to launch a campaign against the precedent of creating such economic structures as ANT.

The logistics of the provocation are not so important for us. More important to understand is who gained from all of this. Who was competing with ANT?

In order to understand the affair more clearly, let us list and compare the opposing forces (see the table on page 126): on the left here are the highest-ranking people involved in ANT; on the right, ANT's main enemies, the direct participants in the attack upon it.

*Yegor Ligachev*
Politburo member
Central Committee
 secretary
Known for his extreme
 dislike of any democratic
 change in the country

*Ivan Polozkov*
First secretary of Krasnodar
 Territory Party
 Committee
Later leader of Russian
 Communist Party
Known for his extreme
 dislike of any democratic
 changes

*Nikolai Ryzhkov*
Prime Minister of the USSR
Known for his dislike of
 democratic programs of
 change in the economy

*Valentin Chikin*
Editor-in-chief of
 *Sovietskaya rossiya*
Known for his extreme
 dislike of democratic
 changes, especially in the
 economy

*Vladimir Ryashentsev*
General director of the
 state cooperative ANT
Has close ties with
 military-industrial circles

*General Dovgan*
General director of the
 military-industrial
 association Vzlyot,
 involved in tank
 manufacturing

It should also be noted that, despite Ryashentsev's claims, ANT was not intending to saturate the market with essential goods. According to published reports, ANT's Western partners were under contract to deliver to the Soviet Union Sony color televisions, Mercedes-Benz cars, and IBM computers—items that were so expensive that the purchasers would obviously be wealthy organizations, not the ordinary citizens of our country. *Nomenklatura* apparatchiks, who did not have to be taught how to make money, began to comprehend the science of how to spend money with taste.[40]

We are not dealing here with a war between democrats and conservatives, but with an internal Party struggle, a battle between clans for spheres of influence in politics, spheres of control in the economy, and simply the opportunity to get their paws on as much as possible.

The creation of this state cooperative and other enterprises with both private and government capital turned out to be an excellent privatization school for the apparatchiks. After all, there was no longer an argument about whether the economy should be privatized, or whether to hold off—of course it had to be privatized. The argument was only about how. The apparat soldiers had done everything to maintain complete control over the production plants in the economy.

One of the last acts of the regime that collapsed in August 1991 was to pass a USSR law "On the fundamental elements of destatification and privatization of enterprises." Under this law, the only legal seller of state property was the USSR Fund for State Property, a government agency. The government anticipated receiving from such sales as much as 450 billion rubles all told over the course of privatization, thus rectifying the catastrophic plight of the economy. But along with this there was another agenda— which, although not publicized, was clear to everyone—to "sell" the property in such a way that the government maintained complete control over it, and above all, control over enterprises. For that purpose, the law stipulated that an enterprise's workers, the members of its labor collective, should be the first in line "to acquire stocks (shares) of the enterprise in comparison with other subjects."[41]

Anyone familiar with the apparat's approach to drafting legislation knows that the constant and persistent emphasis on the perquisites of labor collectives at enterprises can mean only one thing: a collective's exclusive right to be registered as owner of the factory or plant, with no legal opportunity to relinquish its rights to private persons or private capital. But such "collective ownership" is of course only nominal. This right, along with the provision for the entirely cost-free acquisition by the labor collective of the stock package—a right widely ballyhooed by some lovers of humanity among the Party apparat—simply provided the opportunity to preserve the institution of "no one's" property. The administrative apparat would thus remain completely in charge, just as it has always been. It is no accident that this plan received particularly strong support from the directors of enterprises in the military-industrial complex.

Although this law has since been revoked, it should be remembered as a model illustration of the strategy and tactics of the apparat *nomenklatura* in their struggle to keep their power from slipping away.

After the coup, the Russian authorities took a different tack. They endowed all citizens of their republic with equal rights to make investments; citizens are also free to sell off any investments at their discretion. There is hope that such a policy will make it possible to put up to 70 or 80 percent of the shares of major industrial enterprises in the hands of stockholders independent of state officials and other bureaucrats.

But no one can predict for sure whether independence from former government structures will simultaneously mean independence from the shadow, underground structures of power.

# CHAPTER FOURTEEN

*Witness Testimony*

# David Remnick,
# Moscow Correspondent, *Washington Post*

LEV TIMOFEYEV: How long were you in the Soviet Union?

DAVID REMNICK: Three and a half years, from 1988 to 1991.

LT: Did you ever have the chance to meet Soviet gangsters?

DR: You know, I never tried. I think that the language and culture barrier was so great that a meeting with real criminals was impossible. My information about the Soviet mafia is secondhand. But I did write about the shadow economy several times, and when I met with people from those circles, I sometimes felt I was talking to gangsters. But they don't consider themselves to be gangsters.

LT: How did they look, who were these people? What were your suspicions or doubts based on? What made you think these people could be gangsters?

DR: Because they looked like rich people, richer than other Russians . . . it was their style, their way of speaking.

LT: What was that style?

DR: To some extent I had the feeling that they were trying to imitate our mafia—their clothes, for example, and the way they walked. I don't remember all the restaurants I saw them in. There's one on Peace Avenue called Come and Try.

LT: Do you think that people like that could ever take political power in our country?

DR: Well, of course, all my Soviet friends already think that the gangsters are in power.

LT: Your friends think that . . .

DR: That the gangsters are already sitting in some government offices. Of course, I think that, too. I once wrote an article about poverty in the Soviet Union; while I was working on it, I went to Central Asia. I collected some material there about infant mortality, and I had some meetings with the local bigwigs. Of course, I don't know how much these people had in their pockets, but it was obvious. Everyone talked about them as if they were mafiosi. This is hard for a foreigner to understand, because what we know as the mafia and the clans is something completely different. Here, it could just be a chairman of a kolkhoz or the local authority.

LT: What official positions did those mafiosi you met occupy?

DR: They were at the level of the Minister of Health.

LT: The Minister of Health is a mafioso?

DR: I'm really not sure of that . . . I just had a feeling.
Another time I was in Alma-Ata, and I had a meeting with Dinmukhamed Kunayev. After he was forced to retire, he didn't meet with any journalists or foreigners. It was absolutely prohibited. I managed to get a call through to him through some of my new acquaintances, who made the call. You know where he lives? In the same building as the former Party First Secretary; the former Second Secretary; and the current First Secretary, who was Nursul-

tan Nazarbayev at the time; and the current Second Secretary. Four enormous apartments. An amazing building. They still live extremely well. Kunayev had telephoned us earlier to invite us to his home, saying that lunch would be at noon. There were four of us, including Kazakh journalists. We went to the building, but a KGB man stood outside. He said we couldn't meet with Kunayev. "Why?" I asked. "Because Moscow has to decide that. They don't know anything about this in Moscow." Apparently, Moscow didn't want any foreigners to meet with Kunayev. At any rate, it was forbidden for me to see him. We had to go and make some phone calls. I said that I was prepared to give him the questions in advance, and if it was possible, wanted to meet him later in the city.

The meeting took place unexpectedly. I was busy with something else, talking to some people, when I was told that within five minutes I would have a meeting with Kunayev on the street. It was near the Central Committee rest home in a wooded area on the edge of the city. A white Volga came for me. There was a man in the car who looked like someone from the nineteenth century— like an owner of a Southern plantation. Africans would call someone like that a Big Man. He had an amazing hat (like a cowboy's), sunglasses, and an enormous ring on his pinkie. And like an African Big Man, he was carrying a cane. He was an owner of people, this was his land; and you lived, played, and died on his land. For the first time in my life, I understood what that was like. Of course, he was very pleasant, and we had some empty, small talk. People in Alma-Ata love him to this day—a lot of people. He had such authority. People understood that he was the master and they were the slaves. For the first time, I saw people with this kind of outlook.

LT: Authority? In this country, that word has a special significance in the criminal lexicon. It is the *pakhan,* the chief of the band.

DR: No, he was like God with little children. He knew what they were supposed to do. I don't mean everyone in Alma-Ata, but many people. There were more of them than I had thought. I also had a meeting with Geidar Aliyev.* He is now back in Azerbaijan. He has gotten back into politics. But our meeting took place when he was on a pension, and was living very quietly. Once again, some journalist acquaintances helped me to meet Aliyev, at a dacha outside Moscow. Aliyev thought that Gorbachev hated him. It was the first time he was meeting with a foreigner since his retirement, and he spoke openly against the current leadership. It was a turning point for him, that he dared to do this. But his style was not Central Asian. He was dressed differently and behaved differently.

LT: In both Kazakhstan, where Kunayev ruled, and in Azerbaijan, where Aliyev was secretary, there are widespread, divergent mafioso clans. What do those people know about the mafia? Or are they perhaps involved with it themselves? I mean Kunayev and Aliyev.

DR: Of course they know about these clans. And the people who admire Kunayev are aware of his involvement, but do not see any contradictions in that. However, I think that these people don't know what a clan is. I believe only investigators like Gdlyan and Ivanov completely understand what that's all about.

LT: Why did Moscow not allow you to meet with Kunayev? What were they hiding?

DR: You know, it casts a shadow on Gorbachev, when there's a photo where Brezhnev, Aliyev, Kunayev, and Gorbachev are standing together.

LT: Do you have a photograph like that?

*Former First Secretary of the Azerbaijan Communist Party and former Politburo member. —TRANS.

DR: All you have to do is find some magazines like *Ogonyok* or *Soviet Life.* Personal connections, political, government, of course, existed and continue to exist to this day.

LT: Do foreigners living in the USSR feel a danger that these criminal structures will grow so strong that they may throw off any doctrinal cover and start openly resorting to criminal methods of exercising power?

DR: I think you are experiencing the very first stage of capitalism. And it's by no means the best people who are working in favor of its development. The people who ride around in Mercedes-Benzes, who travel abroad, who eat in restaurants, are certainly not the best people of this country. But perhaps that's natural.

# CHAPTER FIFTEEN

# Why Gorbachev?

Gorbachev has gone. But why did he come? Who brought him in? An opinion is going around that in March 1985, Gorbachev was brought to power by a realization in the ruling circles that reform was necessary—above all in the economy. By that time, the rate of growth of the gross national product and productivity of labor had fallen. "Everything is rotten," the best people in the Party, people like Gorbachev and Shevardnadze, had said. "The Fatherland is in danger and the country is on the verge of economic collapse."

But was the crisis in the economy indeed so perilous at the beginning of the 1980s? Haven't Soviet people known worse times, such as the hunger and destruction at the beginning of the 1930s or soon after the war with Hitler? Back then the Communists had not spoken about any special dangers and had not thought of any humane reforms; on the contrary, even during the most disastrous times, they always found reasons for announcing new victories of socialism.

Economic troubles did not alarm the Communists as much as did the political ramifications. "We don't need just *any* growth in the productivity of national labor," said Stalin back in 1929, and his words have not lost their currency even today. "We need a certain growth in the productivity of national labor—exactly the kind of growth that would guarantee the systematic advantage of the socialist sector of the national economy over the capitalist."[42]

Stalin spoke not of the economy, but of power over the economy. At the beginning of the 1980s, his successors were concerned not about the crisis in the economy, but the crisis of power. Behind the phenomenon of increasing economic decline, the Communists—after more than six decades of uninterrupted rule in Russia—were clearly sensing the powerful and growing public opposition to their regime.

We are not talking here about a few dozen dissidents, but the nationwide, daily, pervasive negation of Communist doctrine.

Scholars and sociologists were the first in Party circles to talk about the dangerous growth of opposition, bringing "the human factor" into political currency. This new term was alarming for Communist politicians. In April 1983, Tatyana Zaslavskaya, a leading Soviet sociologist, gave a lecture at a scholarly seminar in Novosibirsk, in which she expressed the idea that the interests of government and society were, if not directly antithetical, at least greatly at odds. These thoughts were a dangerous revelation, even coming from the mouth of one of "their" academicians. Despite the close circle of listeners—among whom were the figures who were to become part of the coming perestroika, like Academician Abel Aganbegyan, economist Boris Rakitsky, Boris Kurashvili, and others—the text of the lecture was confiscated by the KGB.

Nevertheless, Zaslavskaya developed her ideas in subsequent articles, and they illustrated what alarmed the more sensitive adherents of Communist doctrine who were the authoritative government consultants of the time. "Living labor . . . has become a weak point in the functioning of complex technological systems," warned Zaslavskaya. "The average work hour of the modern person is apparently equal to days, if not weeks, of the labor of his parents and grandparents, in the scale of its economic, social, and ecological effect."[43] It was not hard to understand that in exactly the same way, the average work hour of an American or a German was equal to days, months, and sometimes years of labor of a

Soviet person. That meant that the USSR was falling behind the West (or the "socialist sector" was lagging behind the rest of the world) in an increasing geometric progression. A popular joke summarized the situation: "How many years is the USSR behind Japan? Thirty or forty?" "No. An eternity!"

The Communist Zaslavskaya understood this and gave warning:

A highly qualified, socially developed person is a less suitable object of administrative (much less bureaucratic) management. This is one of the reasons why the methods of command administration in the economy and other spheres of life are becoming less effective. . . .

In the 1970s and the beginning of the 1980s, unfavorable tendencies and difficulties arose in the development of the country.

One of these tendencies is the decline in the overall regularity and manageability of social development, which is manifested in the weakening of plan discipline, difficulties in material and technical supply, the emergence of "shadow" economic relations, the growth of some sources of unearned income, and the increase . . . in alcoholism, drunkenness, the weakening of family ties, and so on.[44]

The Communists had always been confident of their power, both over the economy as a whole and over each individual worker. But suddenly, there was some kind of "human factor." Suddenly, an insubordinate person appeared, who refused to obey orders. He, a worker, a subject of "living labor," began to threaten a "decline in regularity and manageability"—or, to put it another way, to threaten the very power of the Communist apparat. What Zaslavskaya was reporting looked very much like a universal quiet rebellion.

Her article was a signal that awareness of the necessity of reform had begun. By the beginning of the 1980s, it had become clear that in some incomprehensible, almost magical way, during relatively peaceful times, and in the absence of overt political struggle, power had slipped out of the Communists' hands. They had not yet lost power over the country as a whole, but they had lost control of the individual worker.

A spontaneous opposition by society was under way, not expressed then or now in any directly political form, but no less real and vigorous even so. It was the opposition of common sense—in the economy, in everyday life, in art, in the public sphere—and it gradually tore apart, dismantled, and brought down the power of Communist doctrine. Although the economic crisis was perhaps clear evidence of the approaching collapse, the main problem for the Communists was that ordinary workers were subverting the rules and laws established by Communist doctrine. That was anything but the desired regularity of planned discipline.

The need for reform arose because the problem of restoring power over the worker was far more important than purely economic indicators. When Gorbachev said that the beginning of reform entirely hinged on his good will—that he could have ruled throughout his long period as General Secretary in the old way—he was prevaricating. If he had not begun the reforms, his term would hardly have been as long. Even if the people would not have openly rebelled, they would have at least given him the silent treatment in the economy and politics. Tension would have increased in society; the sparks of discontent were strong enough to cause an explosion, something like what happened in Romania. Then the Motherland really would have been in danger.

Meanwhile, the methods of naked force against society, and of the Gulag's forced labor (discredited by Khrushchev's revelations), could not be used again. The Communists did not have the force to unleash widespread terror. It was impossible for them to simultaneously wage a war in Afghanistan; maintain a heavy thumb on a Poland in revolt, and keep power in Hungary; support bandit regimes in Ethiopia and Angola; compete with the Americans in the arms race, which was reaching cosmic proportions; and try to squeeze their own country in their fists in the Stalinist way. Even the most hardheaded Communists began to realize that the time had come to seek an accommodation with the people. But the word "reform" itself was not yet uttered; in the traditional Party-bureaucratic lexicon they found a term that was without substance and did not bind them to anything—perestroika.

The political model Communist leaders then dreamed of was something close to fascism—the freeing of economic relations from harsh regimentation while at the same time strengthening political control. This approach could be discerned in speeches of Yury Andropov, energetic though few in number. The people were tired of shortages, and any modification of the Communist system in the direction of economic freedoms would be understood and accepted—even if it was accompanied by a tightening of the screws in politics and ideology. At first glance, it seemed that the only thing lacking to implement this plan was a state idea, a belief in the state's purpose, under the banner of which the political, ideological, and administrative regime could be made harsher.

The Communist idea was no longer good for anything. A return to state terror under the slogan "Forward to Communism!" was now already understood as an absurdity even by the ruling apparat itself, which was increasingly corrupt, and therefore all the more interested in the prospect of a partially free market.

The nationalist Russian idea wouldn't work either. Stalin had exploited it successfully during the war with the Germans. But in a multiethnic empire with a complex set of interethnic problems, a forcible, repressive imposition of this idea would have severe and quite unpredictable consequences and the quiet rebellion against the Communists would turn into a bitter war. It seemed as if the Communist "center" always understood this, and was always afraid of it.

Still, a congenial state idea, suitable for placing at the foundation of a new totalitarianism, did exist, and had existed for a long time—for decades, in fact. Although it was not a nationalist idea, it was a patriotic idea close to it: "The Motherland is in danger!"

From the moment the USSR was created, it was customary to believe that it was living, and would always live, surrounded by enemies. This external danger required the close solidarity of society around the Party and the government. Anyone, therefore, who encroached upon that unity was encroaching on the security of the Motherland. In the official lexicon, the Communist regime and the Motherland were made synonymous. Any attempt to create an opposition political party was thus characterized as "treason against the Motherland." Any dissent—not only in politics but even in philosophy—was viewed as nothing less than "aiding and abetting foreign special services."

By the mid-1970s, this external threat, this "threat of aggression from imperialism" became the chief—if not the only—foundation for Communist state doctrine.

That was how a new escalation of the arms race began, accompanied by equally unprecedented propaganda efforts. Not a word was spoken about the actual aggressive intentions of Soviet foreign policy and Soviet military preparations. Incredibly unscrupulous people were brought into the corps of commentators and international correspondents. Furthermore, in order to prevent unforeseen accidents, the activity of the commentators was strictly controlled through the Department of International Information in the Central Committee of the Party.

This kind of policy forced the USSR to teeter on the brink of war and to wage local wars (as in Afghanistan) in order to maintain an enormous army and to orient its economy accordingly. The military-industrial complex became a much greater political force, since the stability of power depended on it.

By the beginning of the 1980s, it was clear that it was impossible to maintain this military might properly anymore unless a method could be found to eliminate the lag in machine-building,* technology, and the corresponding scientific design. And the lagging behind, as we know, was occurring because the "highly qualified, socially developed person is a less suitable object of administrative (much less bureaucratic) management." Having ceased to be an object of administration, a person became the subject of opposition to the government. And in order to break out

---

*This included manufacturing of nuclear weapons. —TRANS.

of this vicious circle, the military-industrial leaders (Gromyko, Ustinov, and others) summoned to power and supported the youngest, most energetic member of the Communist Party Polit-buro: Mikhail Gorbachev.

The very first perestroika-era slogan was *acceleration*, which meant the priority development of machine-building as the foun-dation of the military-industrial complex. The talk about glasnost, democratization, and so on came much later; many people re-garded such talk just as a political maneuver by the Communists before a new surge of repression and further acceleration of the arms race.

But when Gorbachev opened the era of glasnost and other democratizing (if not democratic) innovations, did he not really understand what he had wrought? Did the "human factor" really not teach him anything? When he proposed a new electoral law in the summer of 1988, did he really not understand that any compe-tition—whether in the economy or in politics—would inevitably lead, not to perfection, but to the complete collapse of Communist doctrine?

No, he understood everything and acted deliberately. He keenly sensed a truth, one that was revealed in the first two years of perestroika and glasnost and that remained inaccessible until re-cently to the thickheaded *nomenklatura* conservatives: it was no longer possible to preserve both doctrine and power over the country simultaneously. The pressure of public opposition would not allow it. The choice was made in favor of preserving power. Gorbachev alone did not make this choice. It was made by the most intelligent and the most flexible—or if you like, the most clever—part of the *nomenklatura*.

Only now do we begin to understand that a revolution occurred in Russia that was unprecedented in the history of humankind. The politicians managed to change state doctrine while preserving their own power. The same ruling structures remained in force, shifting their function slightly in keeping with the new doctrine of market-system and capitalism.

Was it a miracle? There are no miracles in history. And what has happened in Russia is not a miracle, but a logical development, arising out of the covert process of the disintegration of the Communist state system. (It was in fact a covert process, which is why, to this day, it has covert, shadow, secret structures.) Little remained of the "socialist sector of the national economy" (which in fact never existed in a pure form) by the beginning of the 1980s. The whole chain of command of the economy, with all its internal and inter-industrial connections, was corrupt from top to bottom, permeated by relationships to the black market. Paradoxically, the black market maintained a more or less normal production process. It turned out that the capitalist sector that so worried Stalin did not disappear as a result of repression and prohibitions, but miraculously survived and grew within the moribund socialist sector. It became the system of living blood circulation in the dead shell of the planned economy. Were the reforms not made in order to remove the ripening contradiction between the shell and its healthy contents—market relations and private property?

Today moralists are alarmed that yesterday's district committee secretaries will become tomorrow's presidents of banks and commodities exchanges; they fear that the same people will be in charge of all the country's material valuables, only now with the right to private property. Alas, those are the laws of the marketplace; no matter what privatization programs are passed, in the final analysis property will always end up in the hands of the most pushy, unscrupulous, and high-handed dealers. There is nothing that can be done about it. The inevitability of the process (and the neutrality of the economy to moral categories) was expressed well by political scientist Andranik Migranyan: "Whatever should be stolen should be stolen as quickly as possible. That is the only way to stop theft."

In any event, no matter what area of the economy or politics we examine, everywhere we see business being controlled by the same people who were involved in past power structures. The military-industrial complex still has a voice in the economy (in the budget allocation, in particular), in politics, and in the managing of the process of privatization.

President Yeltsin is surrounded by yesterday's *nomenklatura* apparatchiks, just as President Gorbachev was before him. The names are different, but the social profile and political behavior of Yeltsin's personal cabinet are extremely similar to those of Gorbachev's entourage. They are the same provincial Party committee secretaries, making the same efforts to influence the President and thus impede reform in general and privatization in particular.

A memorandum addressed by a group of deputies to both Yeltsin and the parliament states:

Having gained the opportunity to influence policy by extra-political means, essentially the illegal, clandestine, *nomenklatura* bureaucratic means of the past, these apparatchiks cannot help but enter into an unnatural competition (from the perspective of the rule of law) with persons and structures personifying the new democratic policy.

From this point of view, actions planned and carried out with the organizational rapidity customary for the *nomenklatura* are natural:

—forcing into the background colleagues and aides of the President who are not linked with them by previous *nomenklatura* service but have achieved their positions by electoral, democratic struggle;

—taking absolute control over the staffing not only of administrative services but of all state and political institutions;

—blocking the prompt staffing of the State Council, the control administration, and other centers of democratic policy; attempting to isolate the heads and coordinators of these agencies;

—incorporating by fiat a vicious practice whereby decisions of the President on the most important current political matters (including personnel) are prepared clandestinely by a small circle of people who are linked through their common *nomenklatura* past and their incompetence in the matters under review (Yury Petrov, Viktor Ilyushin);

—deliberately concealing from the appropriate state legal

and political analysts the process of drafting these decisions of the State Council.[45]

Communist authority has had three terrible faces, three deadly incarnations: the Party apparat, the military-industrial complex, and the KGB. To this day, these three facets have constantly interchanged or merged into a sort of unity, at times finding themselves in conflict to some degree, but never firmly separating into three. They cannot, finally, divide, because they cannot survive without one another. This three-in-one substantiation emerges in new offices, changes its names, but continues to determine policy, and far from the direction of democracy.

The peculiarity of our time is that the ruling apparat of the past may have rejected its Communist doctrine and previous doctrinal labels, but it has preserved all of its power to distribute material goods in the country. And in the final analysis, he who allocates property calls the political tune. Permission to take part in large-scale enterprise is only granted through these apparatchiks, and only if it is in their interests. The danger isn't that yesterday's district Party committee secretary will become a factory owner or a bank manager. Let him. The trouble is, rather, that this person *is* yesterday's man, an unfree person linked to the conspiracy, bound hand and foot to his social class—that very apparat, military-industrial complex, and KGB. He is dependent on that trinity in everything he does, because he obtains his property rights from them for a price: a silent oath of loyalty. If he breaks that oath, he will not remain a property owner for long.

Have we ended up with democracy? It *seems* that the free market is legal. Fruitful competition is taking shape in small- and medium-scale manufacturing and in the turnover of small and medium capital. Large capital is forming in shares. Smaller and medium-size properties are being transferred to private hands . . . aren't they?

But let us recall that Gorbachev's reforms began for the sake of preserving control over the human being, over the worker. The same people and the same structures are in charge of politics and the economy. Now they have in their hands not the reins of political or administrative power over the individual worker so much as the whip of economic clout, through monopoly control over the system of banks, exchanges, and key sectors of major industry. The influence of large capital over small, the economic leverage of large capital over the proprietor of the workforce and over the individual has been established.

The conflict between power and society has acquired features that, although new for Russia, are entirely traditional for a market economy. As a group of consumers, society is interested in the free play of competing producers, but the monopoly capitalist is concerned with complete control over the economy. The consumer is interested in an abundance of goods and services, in the spontaneous development of production under pressure from public demand. But the monopoly capitalist does not need such unmanageable economic spontaneity; he needs instead as much ordered, tightly controlled production and distribution as possible. This conflict is the economic analogue to the struggle in the political sphere between democracy and authoritarianism or totalitarianism.

In Western societies, such conflicts are constrained by the existence of a powerful, flexible, wonderfully viable middle class. This segment of society, with its inexhaustible entrepreneurial aspirations, is the real motor of market competition and the foundation of political democracy. In Russia today there is no middle class. It is systematically and deliberately destroyed wherever it appears— whether in the form of large-scale farming or embodied in new entrepreneurs in industry, construction, and trade. Many methods are used to kill this class: they include the confiscatory tax policy of the government, the conspiracy of bribe-taking bureaucrats, and the social demagoguery of the defenders of the people's destinies.

Russia does not have the social basis for democracy today. It is deliberately and calculatedly not allowed to emerge. Democracy is being suffocated by the same overt and covert forces that were able to part so cleverly with the dead Communist doctrine while preserving their undivided power over the wealth of the country.

Now they want not only to influence the economy, but to restore their control over society at the previous level.

Apparently they are succeeding. They have learned a great deal. They will allow small property owners the opportunity to feed the country. They understand quite well that it is impossible to reject society's interests directly and crudely. The "human factor" cannot be removed from political calculations, but it seems that it can be manipulated.

Once again, the slogan is resounding: "The Motherland is in danger!" If the danger was fictitious in the past, now it is quite real. The collapse of the former Soviet Union and interethnic and interstate conflicts threaten Russian statehood itself (as well as the republics of Ukraine, Georgia, Uzbekistan, etc.). The economic crisis threatens unpredictable social clashes and disorders—is that not a real danger to the Motherland? The national "Russian idea," which had existed before in the state of some political slumber, has now gained the sacred force of a protective banner.

Perestroika has been successfully completed. All the purposes for which those in power at the beginning of the 1980s were determined to make reforms have now been achieved. Those forces that have held on to the fundamental structures of state power and have preserved their monopoly over running the economy and their control over social processes will establish a regime in the near future in Russia (and in Ukraine, Uzbekistan, and Moldova). As for the kind of regimen, you'll have to judge for yourself. Perhaps the government will be fascistic, or something similar to fascistic. But it's risky to assign labels based on the experience of the past. If the system will be fascism, it will be our peculiarly Russian kind of fascism, something not yet seen in the history of humankind.

"The human factor" is you and I. We will be the Fascists. And we will also be the ones to fight fascism until our last breath.

# Metacorruption

*Anton Koslov**

I.

Everybody in the former Soviet republics is talking and writing about the mafia. Moreover, it seems that any structure can be understood as a mafia, from the KGB to a cooperative selling fruit jam. Shortly before the elections on June 12, 1991, the press published reports that claimed Boris Yeltsin was connected to the Italian mafia. What is important here is not so much the attempt to denigrate Yeltsin as the fact that it was possible to publish such a charge in the mainstream press. The accusation in this case was one of the Party apparat against itself, although it was published in the hard-line Communist newspaper *Sovetskaya Rossiya.* After all, quite "progressive" newspapers have accused a former Polit-buro member, Yegor Ligachev, and other Communists of having ties with the mafia. The very phrasing of the charge is the point here. Not even the fact itself, but the possibility of the fact. Because it places under question not so much the reputation of Yeltsin per se (he has no relationship with the mafia) as the very process of gaining and sharing power in the former USSR. It's implied that he is not connected, but he *could be* connected or he *may be* connected. The presence of this possibility of "being connected" is the chief characteristic of the political process today in the former USSR (the Commonwealth of Independent States?).

*Anton Koslov is a social anthropologist who lives in Paris.

Soviet society is in fact suffering a profound crisis of authority. Everyone now talks about the Communist apparat as a criminal organization. Is this not, however, a simplification of complex social and economic processes under way in the state?

Socialism was the result of an attempt to create a qualitatively new society upon qualitatively new principles; at its foundation supposedly lay noble ideas of freedom and equality. Those who dreamed about Communist society and who began to create it were not criminals, social degenerates, or deviants. Did Dostoyevsky make Raskolnikov a criminal? Were the real-life Nechayev and Dzerzhinsky criminals? Hardly. Then why do criminals, thieves, bribe-takers, and corrupters hold sway everywhere in modern Soviet society?

What is the mafia in the former Soviet Union and the current country (or countries)? Is the very idea of a mafia mistaken? What is it involved in? Drugs? Arms? Prostitution? Gambling? Unlicensed manufacturing and sale? Contraband?

In the broad sense, the mafia is organized crime. In the West, there is a clear definition of organized crime. If we use the definition by U.S. Senators Kenneth McKeller and Frank Lausche, the mafia is an organization whose purpose is systematically to flout constitutional law and order; whose members are involved in gambling, transporting narcotics, extortion, racketeering, prostitution, and other commercial crimes, but who are guided by their own ethical standards; whose members corrupt officials to make their operations easier; and whose leaders maintain authority and discipline within the organization by force.[1]

For the former Soviet Union, such a definition clearly is unsuitable. In the West there is clearly defined legislation, while in the USSR, the line between law and lawlessness was often erased.

One of the most significant aspects of organized crime in the West is the monopolization of the black markets and black economy. The most important factor limiting competition inside the black economy are laws determining which goods and services are legal and which are not. Regulations defining certain production as legal are a kind of tariff. The criminal organization monopolizing the black market depends on the legitimate society, since the black market exists only in contrast with the "white," or legal market. But in the USSR, practically everything can be black market. Soviet criminologists officially report that government bureaucrats do not ask for bribes, they demand them.[2]

II.

In *The Communist Manifesto*, Marx and Engels wrote that the proletariat could become the ruling class only by taking "despotic measures" to change productive relationships and the relationships of property. Such measures were seen by Marx and Engels as a temporary necessity. Lenin extended their thinking; following in Hegel's footsteps, he explained that an idea finds its embodiment in an institution. Marx himself demonstrated that ideas were secondary compared with real activity (and for that reason, the liberation of the proletariat had to be done by the hand of the proletariat itself).

Institution is form, and for the state doctrine of the Communists, form was more important than anything. Without an organization, no Leninism is conceivable. The chief work of Lenin, of course, was *What Is to Be Done?* It predicted everything that would later happen in Russia, from the October Revolution to the Uzbek Cotton Affair and the August putsch. Lenin formulated the necessity of creating a secret organization for the purposes of taking power and establishing a dictatorship. Writing about the Jacobin methods of seizing power he advocated in "Two Tactics for Social-Democratic and Democratic Revolution": "If the revolution ends with a decisive victory, we will settle our scores with tsarism in the Jacobin method, or if you like, in the plebeian method." Later, Lenin quoted Marx, who said that the terror of the French Revolution was a plebeian method to defend revolutionary conquests from numerous enemies.[3] According to Lenin, the Bolsheviks were the Jacobins—or terrorists—of social democracy; the Bolsheviks wanted the people—the proletariat and the peasantry—to settle scores in the plebeian way with the autocracy and with the aristocracy.[4]

Lenin was an advocate of conspiracy. The seizure of power was an act by a secret organization of conspirators and terrorists. This explains his endless harangues against the "legal" Marxists. The legal Marxists advocated *dogovor* (contract) and social evolution. Lenin advocated *zagovor* (conspiracy) and revolution. The contrast between *dogovor* and *zagovor* defined subsequent Russian history.

III.

The organization of a "Party of a new type" is Lenin's main achievement. The essence of the Leninist Communist Party is a system of conspiracy, of conspiracy in the making. Lenin's Party emerged on the political scene precisely during the period when Russia, like the majority of European countries, was on the complicated path of transition from feudalism to capitalism. In fact, the Party itself, and not its ideology, was a reaction of archaic consciousness to the encroachment of the "chaos" of modernism and liberalism. The Bolsheviks seized power in Russia after the bourgeois-liberal, practically bloodless revolution of February 1917. The Russian bourgeoisie turned out to be too dispersed and disorganized to hold on to power or to the historical conquests in the culture of consciousness, which had begun with the reforms of Peter the Great and ended with the triumph of liberalism in 1917.

In the West, the state developed in the direction of *zagovor* to *dogovor*. In this sense, *zagovor* means the concentration of power in the hands of a tiny fraction of society free of all legal restraint, that is, conspiracy. *Dogovor* is the gradual redistribution of capital and power, the increase of awareness of law and the constitutionalization of political and social life, all on a contractual basis. The constitution presented by Oliver Cromwell to the English Parliament was called "the Popular Contract." The contractual nature of civic relations was directly connected with the institutionalization of private property and freedom of conscience.

The right to private property and freedom of religion were the fundamental principles of Western political pluralism; they also served as vehicles of the humanization of social relations and the strengthening of contractual elements of political pluralism. Modern legal norms evolved during the fifteenth and sixteenth centuries and were directly connected with the Reformation and the emergence of capitalism. The Reformation emphasized freedom of conscience, and as a consequence, freedom of speech. For its part capitalism emphasized money and private property. Money is a form of contract, the idea of exchange.

In the eighteenth century Locke and Rousseau spoke of the "social contract." According to Rousseau, human society is built on a contractual basis. By entering society, a person renounces some part of his independence, but assures both security and the defense of his own freedom. Rousseau's ideas were adopted by the founder of the school of classic jurisprudence, Cesare Bonesana di Beccarria, who had a great deal of influence on the formulation of European and American criminal and civil legislation at the turn of the nineteenth century. The culmination of the idea of the contract as the basis of society lies in the U.S. Constitution and the Declaration of the Rights of Man.

Money and property are necessary components of economic development. The Bolsheviks, in seizing power, replaced economic and political relationships built on a contract with economic and political relationships built on a conspiracy. Along with the right to property, the rights to freedom of speech, an independent legal system, and the inviolability of the person and home were lost. The destruction during the Civil War of the class of productive property owners and of the institution of private property led very quickly to an escalation of violence. After all, the primary human property is life, and the primary right is the right to life (including the right to one's own body). Human life and the human body ceased to be property defended by law. Death ceased to be an expression of supernatural will or a tragedy; it turned into a banality, a purely utilitarian and social phenomenon. In September 1918, crowds of Red Army soldiers and their sympathizers walked the streets of Petrograd with a banner on which were drawn an enormous skull and the words "Red Terror!" and "Death to the Bourgeoisie!"[5] Terror was a form of struggle, the substance of which was the opposition of classes. Those who summoned Russia to a Jacobin "plebeian" guillotine did not realize one thing: in the end, form triumphs. In the end, form determines the quality of action and result.

IV.

The organization of the Leninist Party reflected the Leninist culture of consciousness. Lenin was a journalist and conspirator, and in his perception the world consisted of conspiracies of all sorts. Religion was a conspiracy; the government was a conspiracy; the war was a conspiracy; the murder of Volodarsky was a conspiracy;* the rebellion of the *Kronstadt* sailors was a conspiracy.

After Lenin, there was the conspiracy of the Industrial Party. After that was the conspiracy of the Trotskyists. Then the conspiracies of Zinoviev and Co. and the Doctors' Plot. A conspiracy had to be answered with a conspiracy. Thus class warfare was the conspiracy of the proletariat against the bourgeoisie. The Leninist "proletarian" conspiracy begins at the level of language. Lenin was a master at creating new concepts. But he also knew how to imbue old concepts with suitable new meanings. For example, in the Greek *polis* "democracy" meant the participation of all free citizens in the political life of the polis. Democracy was the power of the *demos*, based on universal contractual foundations (or, as we would say now, on a consensus). Since Polybius philosophers have said

---

*V. Volodarsky, the pseudonym of Moisei Goldshtein (1891–1918), a member of the 1905 Russian revolutionary movement and the Communist Party, and a participant in the October Revolution who was murdered by a member of the Socialist Revolutionary Party. —TRANS.

that democracy opposes despotism. However, according to Lenin, "certainly there is *no* principal contradiction between soviet (that is, socialist) democracy and the application of the dictatorial power of individual persons."[6]

From the writing of the first constitutions in Europe and America, the word "constitution" has been understood to mean a supragovernmental document, guaranteeing rights and freedoms, a supreme secular law before which all citizens are equal. But for the Bolsheviks, the Constitution was a screen for conspirators. A resolution of the Eighth Party Congress states: "The functions of Party collectives should in no way be mixed with the functions of state bodies, which are the Soviets. . . . The Party should conduct its decisions through the soviet bodies, within the framework of the Soviet Constitution. The Party endeavors to guide the activity of the Soviets, but not replace them."[7] The Bolshevik language is a new kind of political "language game," a conspirators' code, like those which exist in the criminal world and which are actually one of its prime identifying traits.

At the level of perception and at the level of a new language, conspiracy gained the status of official reality and defined not only the state structure but the entire realm of the new culture (although upon closer examination, the culture was not so new). The construction of society on the basis of a conspiracy led to the formation of the type of culture characterizing archaic societies, built on the principle of family or kin "conspiracy." Interestingly, the "proletarian culture" of the Communist conspirators has many elements similar to those of the traditional culture of the Sicilian mafia. Both are archaic cultures in type, built on the dichotomy of "ours-theirs," when "theirs" is above all a symbol of a system of hostile values.

In such cultures, violence is the main method of resolving internal contradictions. Hence the cult of violence instilled by the Bolsheviks. The Bolshevik language is filled with military terminology. We constantly encounter words like "front," "mobilization," "warriors," and so on. Sentences are put in the imperative form. Combatant language is used even when the subject concerns

peaceful endeavors: "Just as in their day the regiments and battal-
ions were regenerated when the mobilized Communists entered
their ranks, so now all our steam engine and train car workshops,
our railroad depots and offices must be regenerated."[8]

The cult of violence in proletariat culture is fundamental, because
"creative" violence is the only method of transforming society. Class
warfare is a cult of violence. The death of the revolutionary hero in
battle with "dark forces" is a fundamental principle of Communist
pseudo-eschatology; hence the cult of the "mystery." A slogan of
the time was: "The blabbermouth is a treasure trove for a spy!" A
taboo against divulging the secrets of the organization is the very
first condition for membership, and also the first standard of behavior in the context of the general culture of both the mafia and the
Communists. The chief accusation that was made at the Stalinist
trials was espionage on behalf of some foreign country. The divul-
gence of some "secret" was always the greatest crime. One of the
chief heroes of Soviet children's literature, Malchish-Kebalchish, dies
without giving up the famous "military secret."

In Sicily, the key to understanding the culture and ideology of
the traditional mafiosi is the concept of *omertà*, the law of silence
and double standards, where there is one standard of behavior for
family life and quite another for the "outside" world.[9] In dealing
with other mafiosi, each mafioso must be polite, tactful, and cheerfully ready to help if the need arises. However, in dealing with
representatives of the outside world (whether obvious enemies or
ordinary citizens), mafiosi maintain the principle of "false" *omertà*,
according to which all the standards of behavior are only for the
sake of a mask. Sometimes, mafiosi will assure their victims five
minutes before their murder that they are completely safe.[10] The
expression "murder Sicilian-style" means that the murderer and his
victim had trusted relations—the victim trusted the murderer or
the person who brought the murderer to him. Similarly, Bukharin
returned from Paris to Moscow in 1937, under Stalin's assurance
that "we will not let Bukharin come to harm." Soon after his return,
Bukharin was tried and executed.

Another element of similarity between the proletariat and the

mafia culture is the identification of authority with force. All relationships in mafia society are built on respect for force. The
strongest always dominates; even within the patriarchal family,
relations between the father and son are based on force. The
father is the hierarch not by the right of tradition of the patriarchal family structure, but because he is the stronger.[11] Inside
mafia culture great respect is accorded to the individual in whom
both authority and power are concentrated. Where authority and
force are not united in one individual, the person who has more
strength has more authority.[12]

In archaic culture, the cult of force leads to an emphasis on male
qualities of force—bravery, honor, and so on, in contrast to non-
male qualities of weakness, cowardice, etc. This explains the taboo
against homosexuality, since that leads to a loss of male qualities
and, as a result, an atrophy of the male element. The cult of
bodybuilding and sports, both as a mass spectacle and as a means
of training soldiers, has always played an important role in Communist education. Homosexuality is considered an aberration from
the norm and has been punished by imprisonment.

The cult of the maternal and female element is one of the
fundamentals in the culture of the mafia. In the category of things
defining the honor of the mafioso's family, the woman occupies a
special place, since the woman's honor symbolizes the honor of the
family as a whole.[13] In the proletarian culture, the cult of the
"Motherland" always played an important role.

In both mafiosi and proletariat cultures, another fundamental
principle is loyalty to the collective (the new family), not to the
letter and spirit of the law. The law must be broken if it runs
counter to the interests of the collective (the family, the *koski*). The
will of the family (the collective) is higher than the will of any
court.[14] As for blood-relative family ties, in the Leninist vision the
institution of the family is replaced by the institutions of country,
people, Party, collective, army, and so on. As the lyrics of a song
of that era ran, "My country is the kind of country / Where the
whole nation is my family." The linguistic ties of the Communist
"language game" deliberately replace blood and biological rela-

tionships, but meanwhile the nature of the patriarchal society remains essentially the same. Soviet society could be characterized as a mutation of the feudal family, in which, as a consequence of a certain historical divagation, a forcible attempt was made to replace blood ties with grammatical relationships. We recall the tragic story of Pavlik Morozov, the legendary schoolboy who betrayed his father for the sake of the cause, and became a role model in the education of children.

For many years, literacy was a major priority in the Soviet Union. One had to become literate in order to read the works of ideologues and the newspaper *Pravda*. It was no accident that according to Lenin, the work of the conspiratorial organization should be built around *Iskra (The Spark)*, the Party's press organ. Lenin was one of the first to understand the enormous role of the mass media in manipulating the consciousness of the masses. Hence, the universal-education campaign and the struggle against illiteracy.

v.

The reigning ideology is the coded experience of the ruling class. Its main experience is that of the struggle for power, which is subsequently replicated in the structure of social relations. The experience of transition from subordination to power and from the state of being dominated to the state of dominating over others is the chief code which subsequently defines the development of the whole system. If the transition from powerlessness to power is based on conspiracy and the violation of succession and the traditions of political institutions, the entire system of ensuring power will be defined by conspiracy and disruption of succession. This experience is only reproduced further, not modified. The establishment of social relationships on the basis of a conspiracy provides the internal logic for their whole structure. The conspiracy becomes the form immanent in the political organization of society.

During a period of stability, the construction of social relationships on the basis of conspiracy leads to clientalism and corruption. (Clientalism is a form of conspiracy; client relations are of a personal nature rather than an abstract bureaucratic nature and are built on the principle of mutual support. Client relations are characteristic of traditionalist societies. Feudal society was based on the principle of clientalism, according to which all relationships are built around the axis of patron/client and on the personal connection of the patron with the client. By contrast, in modern, industrial society, relationships are built on the principle of universalist standards of bureaucratic honesty. In theory, one's advance up the bureaucratic ladder depends on ability, and distribution is based on need and economic rationality. Nevertheless, clientalism is, of course, still possible in modern society. The difference, however, is that in the feudal society, clientalism is completely acceptable, legal, and based on more or less permanent grounds, while in contemporary society clientalism is not protected by the law and not permanent. The mafia, or the mafia family, is an extreme form of clientalism.)

In a crisis situation, the immanence leads to a new conspiracy. Until the structures that exist under the logic of the conspiracy are destroyed, the conspiracy will constantly reproduce itself.

The Bolshevist conspiracy in politics naturally spread to the economy and to all spheres of social existence in general. Having destroyed the contract-based legal standards characteristic of liberal democracies, the Bolsheviks established conspiratorial legal norms which were essentially a negation of law. Lenin himself demonstrated this in his essay "Extreme Measures of War with Counterrevolution Should Not Be Restricted by Laws."[15] The right to the law became the prerogative of a small group of conspirators. However, the privilege of handling the laws at their own discretion turned out to be only a temporary privilege for many: from Genrikh Yagoda to Lavrenty Beria, from Mikhail Tukhachevsky to Viktor Abakumov, the disposers of human destinies ended their own lives in the stinking cellars of the apparat that they had so faithfully served. That was the logic of the conspiracy: power, based on mutual support and internal Party standards of behavior, with a closed infrastructure that should have been a self-regulating system, but where the only effective regulatory method was terror from above. Terror inside the Party was Leninist self-criticism under a state of siege. Stalin understood this all too well.

Terror is the dynamic of conspiracy, the instrument through which the conspiracy of the minority can be maintained successfully against the majority. Terror synchronizes the work of the system of the conspiracy, supporting it as One Great Conspiracy. Terror coordinates the work of the elements of the conspiracy in time and makes conspiracy effective. In the absence of contractual legal standards and an independent court, the enormous military and economic machinery can function only through centralized terror; besides terror, there are simply no effective levers of governance and control.

Terror becomes a necessity without which the whole machinery starts to break down. For example, the Rosyevsky Factory does not deliver cement on time to Dneprostroy, a construction enterprise. In a country with the rule of law, the owners of the Rosyevsky Factory would pay damages for breach of contract for not delivering their product punctually. In the conspiratorial state, "Comrade Kogan," who serves "under the leadership of Dzerzhinsky" and who knows how to "find the reasons for evil," is dispatched to the Rosyevsky Factory. Upon arriving, Kogan determines the "reasons for evil" and sends Dneprostroy a telegram: "The technical director, the warehouse supervisor, and two expediters have been arrested. Within five hours, seventeen freight cars of cement will arrive at courier speed at Dneprostroy."[16]

Because of terror, the system continues to work, sometimes even with "courier speed." The weakening of terror leads to a desynchronization of the integrated system of the conspiracy, to its fragmentation and the emergence of many medium-size and small conspiracies. It is like a *matryoshka* doll, where each doll contains another, smaller one inside. A conspiracy without terror, the loss of the conspiracy's internal dynamic, leads to a static situation and stagnation. Cesare More, the prefect of the Sicilian police, to whom Mussolini assigned the task of liquidating the mafia, wrote that the reason it was successful in Sicily was the static nature of the social structure. That was exactly what enabled the creation of "a state within a state, with its own laws, taxation system, jurisprudence . . . a regime exploiting the island to the detriment of the state, but in the first place, to the detriment of the population."[17]

Stagnation comes when the sated conspirators have decided that the terror they've imposed has been sufficient, now they can live for a while. But when terror ends, a reverse reaction begins—corruption. The transition from terror to corruption and corruption to terror is the kind of dialectic of rule based on conspiracy. Meanwhile, the conspiracy continues and selective terror is used against those who do not agree to take part in the conspiracy or who refuse to obey the conspirators. That was how it was in the USSR in the period of "stagnation," as the Brezhnev era was called. Besides terror and stagnation (read: corruption), the conspiracy has no alternatives. The alternative can only be a contract which negates the conspiracy, since it means the fulfillment of the law for everyone.[18]

VI.

Corruption and terror can develop parallel to each other, since terror already envisions corruption. With the help of terror, a monopoly is established over the "gift" of the very right to live. Those who have a monopoly on deciding about a person's life also have the right to allocate everything else.

Obviously, even in the Bolshevik Party there were decent and selfless people among the villains. But they were not the ones who set the dominant political tone, a fact that determined the ensuing history of the Party. From its very beginning, the Communist Party was an organization serving the personal ambitions of its leaders. The privileges created by the Bolsheviks, like the distribution of produce and the exclusive vacation homes, were not merely concrete material goods but a way of disseminating prestige. Joining the Party opened up opportunities for social mobility, gaining a new status, and moving up to a new social class.[19]

As Lenin himself said, in 1920, 38 million people were on the government's payroll. That same year, the revolutionary committees and soviets had control over 10,000 state cafeterias. They served only socially reliable citizens.[20]

As one observer pointed out in 1921, "Rarely does a person join the Communists for reasons of conviction; more frequently it is to have power and to plunder with impunity. Meanwhile, they give all of their activity the external appearance of defending the interests of the workers with calls for labor and discipline. . . . All of them usually enjoy special advantages. They receive the best 'shock-workers' rations, demanding that all products be sent to the Communist cells, where they distribute them among themselves without any red tape. They are the first to find out about the appearance in warehouses . . . of scarce items of provision outside the plan and they are the first to grab them. . . . With favoritism, bribe-taking and Party inequality, they have built themselves a tenacious nest in the cooperatives, where now all the managing personnel are Communists. . . . In the area of public health and social security as well, the Communists have aroused the envy and mistrust of the broad non-Party masses. Everyone knows that the resorts in the Caucasus and the southern beaches of the Crimea, supposedly intended for the benefit of ailing members of the proletariat, in fact have been flooded with high-paid Communists and their ladies who try to throw smoke in one another's eyes and who spend their time in endless drinking binges."[21]

A year after the Bolsheviks seized power, in December 1918, at a meeting of the Matovilikhin factory workers, the following resolution was passed: "We demand the immediate removal from the commissars of leather jackets and caps, and that they be used for footwear. . . . We demand that all commissars and employees of Soviet institutions have the same rations as the workers."[22] At the beginning of 1919, Lenin received a telegram from the Sengileyev district of Simbirsk oblast, explaining the reasons for the peasant rebellion in the area: "The representative of the district Party committee participated in . . . dozens of beatings and in the sharing of confiscated items. The Party organization was a tight gang of thieves and White Guard highway robbers."[23] Curiously, in September 1918, immediately after the death of Moisei Uritsky, head of the Petrograd Cheka, at the hands of the poet Kanegisser, rumors circulated that Uritsky had become a millionaire on bribes and thefts. We cannot know whether or not these rumors were true, and it doesn't particularly matter.[24] Uritsky had every opportunity to become a millionaire. In Odessa that same year, the well-known criminal Misha Yaponchik, a repeat offender described in his day by Isaac Babel, commanded the Lenin Regiment while the Odessa Cheka sold cocaine everywhere.

Alas, if the Bolsheviks were merely bandits, that would not be so horrible. No, they were political conspirators and this was not just a conspiracy against power. They were conspirators against society, against history, against life, and against the banality and tautology on which the daily "now" is based.

The Bolsheviks were great specialists in poetic metaphors. A worker had to be "a soldier on the labor front"; a school was a "forge of learning"; capitalism was "devilish interference in social development"; Lenin was "a commander of the new humanity"; and so forth. Plato had exactly such people in mind when he said that poets should be hounded out of the republic, because they lie a great deal and are therefore extremely harmful. Lenin should be considered a Westernizer, not because he read Marx and called for a struggle against "Asianism," but because he was a romanticist of the Western type, a home-grown Russian Novalis, opening, as he himself said, the doors to "a social order which will be capable of creating beauty, immeasurably exceeding everything of which we could only dream in the past."[25]

VI.

Corruption of the apparat began in the first years of the revolution. Even then, the gray masses of functionaries prevailed over the ideologues. The Bolshevist intellectual ideologues found existential liberation in the revolutionary struggle. They believed in their own metaphors. But in the huge territory of the country, they could not help but blend into the mass of functionaries who were so necessary for the new government. Someone gave the order to execute, but someone had to carry it out. The ones who had to carry out orders became, in the end, more powerful than those who gave orders. Lenin wanted to solve the problem of power "in the plebeian style," and for that, "plebes" were necessary.

From the very beginning, the structure of Party authority was filled with people from the lower classes—workers, lumpen, poor peasants, petty civil servants. Before the revolution, these classes had no independent culture of consciousness. Afterward, the only model available to them for self-identification was the familiar one of a semifeudal patriarchal society with its corresponding culture of power. The chief characteristic of the feudal bureaucrat is his dependence on his employer. As Max Weber pointed out, in bourgeois society the government bureaucrat does not view his position, either *de jure* or *de facto,* as a source of constant enrichment. But the feudal bureaucrat sees his position exactly as a source of enrichment. This traditional medieval notion—which epitomizes the quintessential difference between feudal and capitalist principles governing relationships between power and capital—played a significant role in forming the world view of Communist bureaucrat.

Having seized power, these people, who had been "nobodies" only yesterday in the sense of ownership, now were at least distributors, if not owners. Furthermore, by virtue of the drastic change in their social status, they did not have the competence appropriate to their position. The new freedom they had received did not correspond to either their knowledge or their experience.

In their freedom, therefore, they remained as unfree as before. They were the cooks that Lenin had promised to put at the head of the state. For this social group,* which by the end of the 1930s had completely and irrevocably seized complete power in the country, the desire for fullness of life meant not existential liberation through "ecstasy in battle," but a fairly banal possession of power and accumulation of material goods, the maintenance of the material welfare whose distribution they had access to, and voluntarism, barbaric self-satisfaction, and resolute refusal to confront reality. Brezhnev and his comrades-at-arms were vivid examples of such people.

VII.

The terrorist conspiratorial organization concentrated all executive and legislative power in its own hands. It was both the law and the executor of the law. As Lenin wrote: "The difference between proletarian dictatorship and bourgeois is that . . . the former is carried out—and through individual persons—not only by the masses of laborers and the exploited, but also by organizations constructed so as to awaken the masses and raise them up to historic creativity."[26] The law of such an organization is a law unto itself. Therefore, the legal realm of the revolutionary terrorist organization is objectively one of lawlessness.

When terror is stopped and the process of the corruption of the organization begins, what can be seen on its periphery is metacorruption: corruption becomes the norm, and the noncorrupted is viewed as an aberration from the norm. Metacorruption is a stage beyond corruption; it is the corruption of the corrupters, when corrupt power no longer conceals its corruptness. This is the process now under way in the Commonwealth of Independent States. We could say that this is a new form of anomie, anomie

*Known as the *vydvizhentsy,* the workers promoted to administrative posts in the 1930s.

squared. The conspiratorial state could develop only in this direction. Although more than seventy years were needed to dismantle this state, the structure of the conspiracy could not help but collapse.

Everything has its limits. The Leninist conspiratorial norms of state rule do not work anymore. Only the ruling apparat is left, like a kind of metamafia, inside of which is a struggle for power and influence. This struggle is reminiscent of that between the old and new mafias in the West, which finally compelled the mafiosi to reform.

In the West, however, the clashes inside the mafia did not encompass the ruling infrastructure of the whole country, since the mafia did not possess all economic and political power. Many former apparatchiks and KGB officers have turned up in the ranks of the democrats and are jockeying for position using the same kinds of slogans they had so recently suppressed. However much this troubles many people, the plain fact is that it could be no other way: only those who have the necessary economic base for such a fight can scramble to the top. Only the apparat, the former KGB, and the shadow economy have this base. It is therefore not surprising that the chief political players are the same old people. It is just that the more quick-witted and tenacious have replaced those less quick-witted, though no less tenacious.

A battle is under way in the metamafia between conservatives—those advocating preservation of the old order and the traditional, "Sicilian" relationships—and the younger and more energetic, who understand that things simply cannot go on as before. In the 1990s, it is impossible to go on living and functioning with the notions of 1965. Is this not what Eduard Shevardnadze spoke about with Mikhail Gorbachev that memorable day when they decided that "everything is rotten, everything has to be changed"? In the West, the mafia, in order to remain competitive, was forced to undergo perestroika to modernize. Pure parasitism on the body of society was not enough to maintain its viability. From a feudal-corporate organization, the mafia was compelled to turn into a capitalist entity. Perestroika surely occurred, if not glasnost.

In the 1950s in Italy, the status of a mafioso increasingly merged with that of an ordinary criminal. This was largely due to economic and social shifts that occurred in Italian society after World War II.[27] These changes led to the appearance of the so-called entrepreneurial mafia. The mafioso was forced to reincarnate from a feudal patriarch, whose behavior was determined by the parameters of traditional culture, to a capitalist.[28] Transformation and adaptation can be seen in the case of the new "entrepreneurial mafia," but the traditional forms of criminal culture do not disappear in the new conditions of the industrial technocratic society.

What happened in the 1950s and 1960s in Italy is occurring now in Russia. The process is far more painful than in Italy, because the entire society is involved. Sometimes it seems there is not much difference between the simple labor-camp crooks and the arrogant Communist potentates, who are more like the Corleones than like bureaucrats and businessmen. Today, in the CIS, the language of politicians and crooks is the same. This is the consequence of universal impoverishment, the result of that societal "control of everyday life" so effectively created by the Communists. If Lenin could say to Trotsky something like "In his evaluation of tail-endism and national-fatherism, Trotsky is speaking like an arch-revisionist," now Gorbachev says to Igor Boldin, his chief of staff, who came to see him in the Crimea during the coup, "Shut up, you asshole!"[29]

## VIII.

Given this situation, what can we expect? What is happening above largely reflects what is happening below, and vice versa.

Metacorruption has engulfed virtually all segments of society. At the level of the undifferentiated criminal mass, a growth in crime will be observed in connection with the increase in anomie.

In the Soviet Union, anomic tendencies have been observed in society since the beginning of the 1960s; they have been manifested particularly since perestroika. By the end of the 1980s it was clear that Soviet society was drowning in a crime wave. In the first six months of 1989, for the first time in twenty years, more than 1 million crimes were registered; this was 32 percent higher than the same period in 1988. Serious crimes increased by almost 40 percent.[30] The rise has affected all the former republics. In the first three months of 1991, the number of severe crimes increased 20 percent over the same period in 1990. Lithuania and Estonia registered the greatest growth of crime.[31]

The penetration of the southern mafias will continue in the northern regions. It is well known that Chechen, Azerbaijani, Armenian, Korean, and other mafias operate in Moscow and in other major cities. (Interestingly, in Moscow there exists a criminal group of deaf-mutes, the most reliable type of gang in terms of keeping secrets.) All of these organizations have their contacts in the power structures and law-enforcement agencies and are catalysts in the process of corruption of power structures. The process was similar in Italy in the 1960s and 1970s.

The infiltration of domestic criminal groups into foreign countries is already going on and will continue. In the United States, Germany, and Israel, there are criminal gangs among Soviet émigrés. No doubt the flow of capital abroad will begin (if it hasn't already), and will partially penetrate the "black" economy of Western countries. Why should mafioso millionaires stay in cold and hungry Russia when they can transfer abroad first their money and then themselves?

As a consequence of the increasing anomie, there will be an overlap of organized crime with youth crime. In 1988, 18,000 members of young gangs were listed in police records, and that is only a drop in the ocean. The Solntsevo and Lyubertsi Moscow suburban youth gangs and the teen gangs of Kazan have received much press coverage. In the last twenty years, youth crime increased 50 percent, nearly doubling among teenagers.[32] In 1988, every seventh criminal apprehended in the USSR was a minor, and every fifth criminal was in the eighteen to twenty-four age group. People under twenty-nine make up 57 percent of all criminals. Interestingly, in the mafia-type crimes like racketeering, a third of the criminals were minors.

The rise in youth crime may be a side effect of the demobilization of the army. It is known that in 1918 in Sicily, the activation of the mafia was fostered by the demobilization after the war. As a consequence of this postwar influx of soldiers, who often brought their weapons home with them, the level of violence in Sicily increased sharply.[33] A similar situation may be created in the former USSR as armed forces return from Eastern Europe.

Unquestionably the quantitative spurt in crime influences the nature of crime. After World War II mafia criminal organizations experienced changes in both Japan and Italy. This process could be characterized as the "gangsterization" of the mafia. The dominant model became the North American mafia, which gangsterized at the end of the 1920s and the beginning of the 1930s. While the American mafia, in internal structure, culture, and composition, is an outgrowth of the Italian mafia, in general it is a completely separate organization that emerged in completely different conditions.[34] The distinguishing features of the new mafia were its corporate structure and urban nature.

The Sicilian mafia underwent similar changes after the war. In the traditional society in Sicily and in urban ghettos, the mafioso played the role of a middleman in a geographically restricted district. But the modern mafia was a reaction to specific changes in market and legal relationships in society. Apparently, something similar should be expected from criminal-mafia groups in the former Soviet Union. Given their numbers, the opportunities presented by the transition to the free market, and a relatively easy access to weapons, we can only guess at the scale of gangster wars to come in the CIS.

Clearly, the wave of ordinary crime cannot help but influence the growth of political crime in the country.

Ethnic conflicts will also foster the rise in crime. In many regions, criminal groups stimulate such conflicts in order to increase their influence. The declaration of independence of the republics may serve only as a smoke screen for the preservation of old mafioso-clientalist Party apparat structures. The political conflicts within such republics may be a cover for power struggles among various mafias. In Italy, the mafia speaks out with slogans for regional independence, nationalism, and rejection of so-called northern Italian colonialism. In Georgia, one opposition leader had the title *vor v zakonye* (literally, "thief in law"), a sign of recognition and respect in the underworld for someone who observes the rules of the underworld code. Ex-President Zviad Gamsakhurdia called all of his opponents protégés of Moscow and the "Moscow mafia."

There will be a regrouping in the power apparat as well as the appearance of new clientalist structures from the old ruling apparat under new political slogans. The old apparat will not go anywhere. In industrially developed regions of the European part of the former USSR, in Siberia, and in the Far East, the old power structures will merge with the new technocratic class while preserving the old system of client relationships. In some cases, the old apparat will melt into a new "entrepreneurial" mafia, similar to the one that formed in Italy in the 1960s. The mafia, after all, is nothing other than clientalism brought to its logical conclusion. Modern clientalism can link parliamentary factions, political parties, and ministries, and it can hide under the names of various civic organizations. The appearance of entire clientalist factions is possible, which will go into various institutions. These factions will not be ideological; their only purpose will be to increase their influence. With the changes in the ruling structures, both old and new forms of corruption will flourish.

The mafia's access to unlimited finances and its foreign currency reserves will enable it to partially control the ruling structures by financing them. There will be a penetration of criminal elements into new political structures. In the USSR, as in Italy, the mafia in recent decades managed to accumulate gigantic capital. Many mafioso have become millionaires in the last few years. Mafia entrepreneurs have gained access to the world of high finance and politics. In southern Italy, these entrepreneurs are a new elite, pushing the old latifundia aristocracy into the background with the entrepreneurial class that grew rich during and after the war. Many representatives of these two classes holding political and economic power in southern Italy were forced to settle in other regions of Italy in order to save their lives. Something similar is happening in the south of the old USSR. In the southern republics, political alliances with the mafia are advantageous because the mafia is the only real authority. By influencing the economic development of the region, the mafia obtains the necessary political influence.

Another way for the mafia to take part in political life is to form lobbying groups and subsequent coalitions with other political organizations, thus penetrating the polity. In Italy, the lobby created by the mafia at times forms close ties with the major political industrial lobby. There was the story of Michele Sindona, a Sicilian financier who was connected both with various mafia groups and with the faction of Giulio Andreotti, the former Premier. If something like this can happen in Italy, it is all the more the case in Third World countries, where the political parties work closely with criminal organizations. Thus in 1981, a member of the Libyan parliament, Mohammed Delal, sold 200 kilograms of heroin to the New York mafia.[35]

In Italy, the mafia penetrates all major parties, from the Christian Democrats to the former Communist Party. In major U.S. cities, the mafia sometimes had ties to the Democratic Party.

Some parts of the former Union's economies have already fallen under control of purely criminal structures, and some criminal and semicriminal structures have been created especially to run the economy. Entire spheres of entrepreneurship have emerged under mafia patronage. The sale of computers is one of them.

In the poorly developed southern regions, what may be called "mafia enterprise" has begun to emerge. We know that in Italy a merging of the traditional culture of the mafia with the culture of capitalism spawned numerous enterprises of this type. Mafia enterprise tries to monopolize the market, through threats and by employing violence directly. Besides the takeover of the markets, another important source of profits for the mafia is the lowering of wages of workers at enterprises they control, with a high turnover of the labor force. The mafia decreases wages by not paying for social insurance, not paying overtime, and simply cutting salaries. It thus resembles early capitalist employers of the European Industrial Revolution. Similar tendencies may occur in the former USSR in the near future, with unemployment expected to reach 10 percent if the ruble is converted.[36]

It is quite obvious that with privatization and capitalization, the mafia will be doing battle with the trade unions. The mafia has a long history of warring with labor movements. As a rule, it was an opponent of syndicalism. In our day, at enterprises that have fallen under mafia control, unions are usually liquidated or their leaders become mafia people. A similar phenomenon can be observed in all the former Communist regimes and in totalitarian regimes in general. Interestingly, during the beginning of the Fascist government's campaign against the Mafia in 1922, some Sicilian newspapers wrote that it had definitively put an end to the Mafia, since two identical institutions—that is, the mafia and the Fascist government—could not exist in one place.[37]

Control over the labor market is a very important aspect of the mafia's monopolization of certain spheres of entrepreneurial activity. For example, in Italy, the mafia, by escalating threats and by violence, blocked the construction of a tourist complex for UN workers on the Ionian coast near Reggio; it feared losing its monopoly over the labor market there.[38]

With the extension of foreign trade, Western mafia capital has begun to penetrate the Soviet economy. One incident involved Filshin, then deputy prime minister of Russia, who had approved a deal between the Dove Trading Corporation, registered in South Africa under the name Colin Gibbons, and the government of the RSFSR. In exchange for consumer goods totaling $1 billion, the government of the RSFSR was supposed to pay Gibbons 140 billion rubles (roughly the annual budget of the USSR Ministry of Defense). If Filshin is to be believed, this money was supposed to be invested in an oil refinery near Irkutsk. According to information from the Swiss police, the whole deal was closely connected to an attempt by the Medellín cocaine cartel to launder some of its money.[39]

VIII.

On August 21, 1991, the Communist regime fell, but metacorruption remained. The system of endless conspiracies was in place. New conspirators are struggling for power. Metacorruption is the logical development of the system of the Bolshevik conspiracy—the policy according to which the powers that be "should stand for ruthless, firm power, for a dictatorship of certain individuals."[40]

The Communist corruption of state and society is the consequence of the disintegration of the very process of the comprehension of reality. The Leninist Communist project is like a sick fantasy of bliss after death, stripped of its religious content.

A way out of the impasse of metacorruption, both economically and morally, is possible only through a revolution in people's minds—an aesthetic, ethical, and religious revolution. The emancipation of thought is necessary. Thought in fact is the microstructure of power; without changing it, it is impossible to change the macrostructure of power. Emancipation of thinking is needed because only then is a way out possible from the dead-end paradigms of false theory. True liberalism, economic and legal, begins where conspiracy ends and a contract starts that is not only social but also "natural."

The way out of metacorruption lies in liquidating the structures of conspiracy and returning the contractual foundations of economic and state governance. Private property must be restored, since only by restoring an institution of property is the creation of a true rule of law possible. This is confirmed by the entire experience of the development of European civilization, and this experience ought not to be rejected.

1. Obshchestvenno-politicheskiy klub "Alternativa," "Tenevaya ekonomika: Korni, mashtaby, ugroza" [Alternative Social Political Club, "Shadow Economics: Roots, Scale, and Threat"], *Positsiya*, no. 1, January 1991.
2. *Twentieth Century and Peace*, no. 4, 1990, p. 39.
3. *Izvestia*, June 22, 1991.
4. Interview of Tatyana Koryagina by Lev Timofeyev, July 1991.
5. See Lev Timofeyev, *Ya-osobo opasny prestupnik* [I Am an Especially Dangerous Criminal], *Vsya Moskva*, 1991, p. 101.
6. *Izvestia*, October 25, 1991.
7. *Argumenty i fakty*, no. 52, December 1991.
8. Raisa Gorbacheva, *Ya nadeyus* (Moskovskaya Kniga, 1991), p. 125. Published in English as *I Hope* (HarperCollins, 1991).
9. "Grustnyye popytki Vitaliya Koroticha" ["The Melancholy Endeavors of Vitaly Korotich"], interview of Vitaly Korotich by E. Dodolev, *Moskovsky komsomolets*, September 21, 1991.
10. E. Gierek, *Vospominaniya* [Memoirs], *Argumenty i fakty*, no. 4, 1990.
11. Yegor Ligachev, *Vospominaniya* [Memoirs], *Argumenty i fakty*, no. 4, 1991. Published in English as *Inside Gorbachev's Kremlin* (Pantheon, 1993).
12. Ligachev, *Vospominaniya*, *Argumenty i fakty*, no. 6, 1991.

13. *Ibid.*

14. Telman Gdlyan, "Piramida" ["The Pyramid"], *Strana i mir*, no. 3, 1989, pp. 58–63.

15. *Ibid.*

16. *Ibid.*

17. See, for example, Dmitry Likhanov, "Koma," *Ogonyok*, no. 3, January 1989.

18. Boris Yeltsin, "Ispoved na zadannuyu temu" ["Confession on an Assigned Theme"], *Pik*, 1990, p. 78. Published in English as *Against the Grain* (Summit Books, 1990).

19. I. Usmankhodzhayev, *Prodolzhaya delo Oktyabrya* ["Continuing the Cause of October"], *Kommunist Uzbekistana*, no. 11, 1987, p. 4.

20. *Ogonyok*, no. 14, 1989.

21. Chris Ogden, "Maggie: An Intimate Portrait of a Woman in Power," *Inostrannaya literatura* [Foreign Literature], no. 4, 1991, p. 91.

22. "Grustnyye popytki Vitaliya Koroticha," ["Melancholy Endeavors of Vitaly Korotich"], E. Dodolev.

23. *Izvestia*, January 11, 1992.

24. *Moskovsky komsomolets*, March 6, 1991.

25. *Ibid.*

26. Leon Onikov, *Ya obvinyayu* [I Accuse], *Pravda*, October 7, 1991.

27. *Moscow News*, no. 39, September 29, 1991.

28. *Argumenty i fakty*, no. 39, 1991.

29. Andrei Sakharov, *Vospominaniya* [Memoirs], *Znamya*, no. 3, 1991, pp. 104–5. Published in English as *Memoirs* (Knopf, 1990).

30. *Izvestia*, December 31, 1991.

31. *Ibid.*

32. *Komsomolskaya pravda*, July 5, 1991.

33. *Moscow News*, November 18, 1990.

34. *Argumenty i fakty*, no. 5, 1991.

35. *Komsomolskaya pravda*, October 31, 1991.

36. *Komsomolskaya pravda*, December 7, 1991.

37. *Ibid.*

38.  *Izvestia,* November 4, 1991.

39.  *Moscow News,* April 1, 1990.

40.  *Izvestia,* April 23, 1990.

41.  *Komsomolskaya pravda,* July 5, 1991.

42.  Joseph Stalin, *Sochineniya* [Works], vol. 12, p. 79.

43.  Tatyana Zaslavskaya, "Tvorcheskaya aktivnost mass: Sotsialnyye rezervy rosta" ["Creative Activity of the Masses: Social Reserves of Growth"], *Eko,* no. 3, 1986, p. 6.

44.  *Ibid.,* p. 8.

45.  *Moscow News,* September 29, 1991.

## NOTES FOR AFTERWORD

1.  Donald Cressey, *Criminal Organization: Its Elementary Forms* (Heinemann Educational Books, 1972), p. 84.

2.  See article by Gurov in the anthology *Pogruzheniye v tryasinu* [Sinking into the Quagmire] (Progress, Moscow, 1991).

3.  Karl Marx and Friedrich Engels, *Le Manifeste du parti communiste* (Paris, 1986), p. 86; V. I. Lenin, *Deux tactiques de la social-democratie* (Paris, 1971), pp. 67–70.

4.  *Ibid.*

5.  A photograph of this was published in the newspaper *Vooruzhyonny narod,* Petrograd, September 1918.

6.  V. I. Lenin, *Polnoye sobraniye sochineniy* [Complete Works], vol. 36, p. 199.

7.  *KPSS v rezolyutsiyakh* [Resolutions of the CPSU], Moscow, 1983, vol. 2, p. 108.

8.  *Pravda,* March 20, 1920.

9.  See Herner Hesse, *Mafia and Mafiosi: The Structure of Power* (Saxon/Lexington Books, 1973), p. 26; and Anton Blok, *The Mafia of the Sicilian Village, 1860–1960* (Harper & Row, 1973), p. 173.

10.  Blok, *Mafia of the Sicilian Village.*

11.  Pino Arlacchi, *Mafia Business* (Verso, 1980), p. 4.

12.  F. Ianni, *The Family Business* (Russell Sage, 1972), p. 13.

13. Arlacchi, *Mafia Business*, p. 8.
14. See Shvedov in the anthology *Pogruzheniye v tryasinu.*
15. Lenin, *Polnoye sobraniye sochineniy*, vol. 37, p. 129.
16. V. Yurezansky, *Pokoreniye reki* [Conquest of the River] (Moscow, 1946), pp. 172–75.
17. A. Folcionelli, *Les Sociétés secrètes italiennes* (Payot, 1936), p. 222.
18. Interestingly, Mafia enterprises in southern Italy were a model of authoritarian organization similar to Stalin's. See Arlacchi, *Mafia Business*, pp. 91–92.
19. For the lower classes, criminal organizations often open up opportunities for social advancement that are not possible in the context of legitimate society. In Italy, the mafiosi were from the peasantry and made up the new Sicilian middle class.
20. N. Bugai, *Chrezvychaynyye organy sovetskoy vlasti* [Extraordinary Agencies of Soviet Authority] (Moscow, 1990), p. 229.
21. A. Terne, *V tsarstve Lenina* [In Lenin's Tsardom] (Berlin, 1922), pp. 52–54.
22. Documents cited in *Moscow News*, nos. 10/11, 1991.
23. *Ibid.*
24. See *L'Illustration*, October 12, 1918.
25. *Perepiska Lenina s Lunacharskim* [Lenin's Correspondence with Lunacharsky] (Moscow, 1971), p. 46.
26. Lenin, *Polnoye sobraniye sochineniy*, vol. 36, p. 99.
27. Arlacchi, *Mafia Business*, p. 59.
28. *Ibid.*
29. *Time*, October 7, 1991.
30. *Pravda*, August 12, 1989.
31. *Libération*, August 8, 1991.
32. *Sovetskaya molodyozh* (Riga), June 28, 1991; *Agitator*, no. 13, July 1989; *Sotsialisticheskaya industria*, no. 110 (6001), May 13, 1989.
33. Christopher Duggan, *Fascism and Mafia* (Yale University Press, 1988), p. 107.
34. See Donald Cressey, *Theft of a Nation* (Harper & Row, 1969), pp. 37–47.

35. Arlacchi, *Mafia Business*, p. 192.
36. *Libération*, September 23, 1991.
37. Duggan, *Fascism and Mafia*, p. 100.
38. Arlacchi, *Mafia Business*, p. 97.
39. *Les Échos* (Paris), February 19, 1991.
40. Lenin, *Polnoye sobraniye sochineniy*, vol. 36, p. 206.

Lev Mikhailovich Timofeyev was born in Leningrad on September 8, 1936. In 1958, he received a degree in international economics from the Moscow Foreign Trade Institute. He worked for several years in foreign trade, as a sailor and as a military translator.

In 1978 he published *Technology of the Black Market (Or the Peasant's Art of Starving)* while working for the magazine *Molodoi Kommunist*. From December 1987 until October 1990 he was publisher of the journal *Referendum*, which confirmed his position as one of the leaders of the democratic movement in the Soviet Union. His poetry, essays, short stories, and literary criticism have appeared in the publications *Yunost*, *Smena*, *Teatr*, *Oktyabr* and *Novy Mir*. In 1991, he edited the anthology *The Anti-Communist Manifesto: Whom to Help in Russia?*, published in the U.S. by Free Enter Press, and his book *I Am an Especially Dangerous Criminal* was published in Moscow.

A NOTE ON THE TYPE

The text of this book was composed in a version of Palatino, a typeface designed by the noted German typographer Hermann Zapf. Named after Giovanbattista Palatino, a writing master of Renaissance Italy, Palatino was the first of Zapf's typefaces to be introduced in America. The first designs for the face were made in 1948, and the fonts for the complete face were issued between 1950 and 1952. Like all Zapf-designed typefaces, Palatino is beautifully balanced and exceedingly readable.

Composed by The Haddon Craftsmen, Inc.,
Scranton, Pennsylvania

Printed and bound by
Fairfield Graphics,
Fairfield, Pennsylvania

Designed by Mia Vander Els